NOT SO FAST

NOT SO FAST

Parenting Your Teen Through
the Dangers of Driving

TIM HOLLISTER AND
PAM SHADEL FISCHER

Foreword by Deborah Hersman, President,
National Safety Council

REVISED AND EXPANDED SECOND EDITION

CHICAGO
REVIEW
PRESS

Published by Chicago Review Press Incorporated
814 North Franklin Street
Chicago, Illinois 60610
ISBN 978-1-61373-899-3

Library of Congress Cataloging-in-Publication Data
Names: Hollister, Tim, 1957– author. | Fischer, Pam Shadel, author.
Title: Not so fast : parenting your teen through the dangers of driving / Tim
    Hollister and Pam Shadel Fischer ; foreword by Deborah Hersman, President,
    National Safety Council.
Description: Revised and expanded second edition. | Chicago, Illinois :
    Chicago Review Press Incorporated, [2018] | Includes index.
Identifiers: LCCN 2017020802 (print) | LCCN 2017057120 (ebook) | ISBN
        9781613739006 (adobe pdf) | ISBN 9781613739013 (epub) | ISBN
9781613739020
    (kindle) | ISBN 9781613738993 (trade paper)
Subjects: LCSH: Teenage automobile drivers. | Teenage automobile
    drivers—Attitudes. | Automobile driving. | Distracted driving. | Parent
    and teenager. | Traffic safety.
Classification: LCC HE5620.J8 (ebook) | LCC HE5620.J8 H65 2018 (print)
| DDC
    629.28/30835—dc23
LC record available at https://lccn.loc.gov/2017020802

Cover design: Rebecca Lown
Cover illustration: Nancy Diamond
Interior design: PerfecType, Nashville, TN

Printed in the United States of America
5 4 3 2 1

In memory of Reid Hollister, 1989–2006

With love for our children,
Martha Hollister and Zach Fischer

Donation of Book Proceeds

Proceeds from the sale of this book benefit the Reid Hollister Memorial Fund, which is part of the endowment of the Asylum Hill Congregational Church in Hartford, Connecticut, and traffic safety programs. At the time of his death, Reid was a Sunday school teacher at Asylum Hill, beloved by kindergartners and first graders. Reid's Fund benefits infant and toddler education in the City of Hartford.

Not So Fast in Spanish

Not So Fast, first edition, has been published in Spanish under the title *No Tan Rápido* (Chicago Review Press, 2015) and is available through bookstores and online retailers.

Not So Fast on YouTube

With financial assistance from the Travelers insurance company, a six-minute video summarizing *Not So Fast*'s key lessons for parents is available on YouTube: www.youtube.com/watch?v=QmCJKvyXhEQ.

CONTENTS

FOREWORD

Reading this book is a down payment on your teen's life. We don't talk about it enough, but the riskiest thing we let our kids do is get behind the wheel of a car. Motor vehicle crashes are the number-one killer of teens, and as parents we are the first line of defense.

Like many parents picking up this book, I am eager to keep my kids safe. As a mother of a seventeen-year-old new driver and his two younger brothers, I openly share in every parent's anxiety in prepping our children for the dangers of driving. As the president of the National Safety Council, my job is to share safety trends and statistics—and when it comes to teens and driving, they aren't good. When I was in high school, we were automatically enrolled in mandatory driver's education and couldn't wait to gain our independence to join friends cruising on Friday nights. Today, many schools have cut back on driver's education, and teens are waiting longer to get licensed. In some cases, these delays are counteracting graduated driver licensing laws that keep teens safer on the road during that critical first year behind the wheel. Whether your child is fifteen or eighteen, he lacks experience driving and needs you to be involved in this critical life skill development, even if he delays licensure.

The good news is that since I learned to drive, teen fatalities have been reduced by 50 percent, thanks in part to the effective advocacy and tireless dedication of grieving parents like Tim Hollister and lifelong road safety warriors like Pam Fischer, who lay out many hard-learned lessons in the pages to come. The bad news is that in recent years we've seen teen deaths rising again, and we know that almost half of all teen drivers will experience a crash before graduation. Modern-day distractions make driving even more dangerous, even while new safety features in cars abound. As Tim writes, it's important to understand the changes in our social and technological environment if we are to keep our kids safe.

Parents have all heard the old adage "Do as I say, not as I do," but our children have been watching us since they were babies, and they do what we do. You play a crucial role in training your teen, not just when she is preparing for her driving test but also when she's learning what not to do while behind the wheel, how to manage passengers, and how to use or misuse the technology in her hand or at her side as she drives. These are just some of the straightforward and digestible lessons imparted in *Not So Fast*. While our kids may not always appear to be focused on us, research shows that parents can make a significant dent in the odds of their teen being in a crash, by exhibiting the right behaviors and enforcing the simple guidelines Tim and Pam set out.

Sadly, it is parents like Tim, who've lost their son or daughter to a motor vehicle crash, who make the best teachers. Rather than taking cues from state laws that establish the minimum level of safety, and friends and neighbors who don't fully recognize the dangerous pitfalls, you have the chance to learn from Tim and Pam, experts who gracefully and knowingly outline the best way to parent a new driver in this easy-to-read book.

I am so grateful to them for providing this great roadmap for parents. There is nothing more important to teens' safety and well-being than teaching them to be safe drivers. I know you are busy and have many things that demand your attention, but please spend ten minutes and read one chapter every night; it is a down payment that will pay dividends for years to come.

—Deborah Hersman
President
National Safety Council
Itasca, Illinois
August 2017

AUTHORS' NOTE

In this book, *teen* primarily refers to those fifteen to twenty years old. Writing this book, we debated whether to refer to teens as *kids* or *children*. We recognize that every teen is different, and while some are frighteningly unready to drive at age sixteen or seventeen (or twenty-one or twenty-five), some are levelheaded and careful at fifteen. Rather than painting anyone with an unfairly broad brush, we use *teen* in both the gender-neutral and maturity-neutral senses.

Recognizing that many teens are supervised by someone other than a biological or adoptive parent, when we say *parent* we mean any adult who supervises a teen's driving (and in our model teen driving agreement, we use the term *supervising adult*).

The National Highway Traffic Safety Administration and traffic safety advocacy organizations avoid the term *accident* and use *crash* to emphasize the fact that more than 90 percent of what happens on the road is the result of what someone did or did not do, and therefore was preventable. We agree, and use *crash*.

We have referred to statistics sparingly, and when we have, they should be regarded as highlighting a range or order of magnitude only. Crash data are finalized about two years after the fact, and electronic reporting of crashes continues to evolve slowly. Moreover, while fatality statistics tend to be fairly precise, data about crashes, injuries, and costs are not uniformly reported or counted, and thus such numbers should be regarded only as indicative of trends and magnitudes.

This book is evidence based and draws upon research from respected academic and professional sources; however, it is not an academic report and therefore does not contain specific citations but rather a teen driving resource section, which lists the organizations whose work has provided the information cited.

"Not So Fast, Young Man/Lady"

Tim's seventeen-year-old son Reid died in a one-car crash on an interstate highway in Connecticut in December 2006, eleven months after receiving his license. In 2007, Connecticut's governor asked Tim to serve on a task force charged with overhauling the state's then very lenient teen driver law. In the course of that work, Tim learned that during those months in 2006, like so many other parents, he had not been well informed about the risks and dangers of teen driving—in part because much of the literature available to parents doesn't fully describe the dangers of teen driving and what parents can do to counteract them. Most articles, handbooks, and manuals, Tim discovered, tell parents that their job is to teach their teens the rules of the road, how to handle a car, and how to avoid hitting anything, but the literature omits or passes lightly over the many things that parents need to do *before* teens get behind the wheel.

Pam, a nationally known traffic safety professional, author, and advocate, is the mother of Zach. Despite serving as her state's highway safety director and being widely known as "the Safety Mom," when Zach got his license in August 2012, Pam worried just as much as any parent, if not more due to her knowledge of the dangers of teen driving. Five months later, Zach was involved in two crashes—thankfully, vehicle damage only—in a span of nine days.

Pam's experience highlights the fact that even a traffic safety expert's teen driver is vulnerable to crashing. That's because teen drivers are inexperienced and do not have the skills needed to recognize a hazard and take corrective action. At the same time, their brains are not fully developed until they reach their early to midtwenties, which explains why they do not process or recognize risk the same way adults do. Parents need to understand this and recognize that even good intentions and lots of practice, while helpful, do not guarantee a crash-free teen driver.

And that is what prompted this collaboration. While our work in teen driving had different starting points and has taken different paths, our efforts converged in advocacy and our agreement about a troubling gap in the national literature: why and how parents should manage their teen drivers day by day before they get behind the wheel. Teen licensing laws are based on solid evidence of what restrictions reduce the high crash risk for novice drivers, but these laws don't come with instructions for parents. This book, derived from our parallel and common experiences, from both tragedy and analysis, is an effort to fill this hole.

When the first edition of this book was published in 2013, teen driver crash rates and fatalities had been declining for more than a decade. This was the result of states adopting stricter three-stage teen licensing laws, a trend that coincided with an economic downturn and a drop in both miles driven by teens and the number of teens obtaining a license. Numerous studies have confirmed that teens were negatively impacted by the recession of 2007–2012, when the cost of owning and operating a vehicle became more of a hardship. Families affected by the recession were less able or willing to subsidize driving costs for their teens, further impacting teen licensure rates. More recently, however, as the economy has improved and gas prices have fallen, more people, including teens, are driving more—and therefore more are dying on the nation's roadways. In 2015, fatal crashes involving teen drivers increased 11 percent over the previous year. Teen driving remains a national public safety crisis—thus the need for better parent education.

In these pages, therefore, parents will find topics infrequently discussed in most teen driver education materials and never before pulled together in a single resource, including:

- the characteristics of teens and new drivers that make them crash-prone and that, unfortunately, cannot be overcome with training and good intentions
- why driver education (driver's ed), while essential to learning to operate a vehicle, does not overcome the primary causes of teen driver crashes
- how parent attitudes compound the risks
- when a teen is ready, as opposed to eligible, to drive
- why strict teen licensing laws work
- how to get teen drivers to heed safety warnings
- the critical difference between purposeful driving and joyriding
- how to negotiate and enforce a parent-teen driving agreement that targets and preempts the riskiest situations

- how to handle the car keys
- why passengers, including siblings, increase teen crash risk
- how to manage curfews
- how to use traffic tickets as teachable moments
- the hidden dangers of buying a car, "connected car" technology, headphones, and student transportation permission forms
- why the price of gas is a curse and a blessing
- why zero tolerance for electronic distractions and impaired driving (drunk or drugged) is essential
- whether teens should use GPS
- how to use technology to track a teen's driving
- how lack of sleep impacts driving, and how to prevent teens from driving while drowsy
- what high schools can do
- supervising other people's teen drivers
- the special challenges of teen driving faced by single parents and non-English-speaking households

This is, therefore, a unique and somewhat odd book for parents of teen drivers, because it contains almost nothing about how to teach a teen to drive a car. We are not driving instructors, and teaching teens how to operate a vehicle is only part of keeping them safe; the other part is parent supervision and oversight. Our exclusive focus is helping parents make informed decisions about whether, when, and how their teens should drive in the first place, both initially and day to day. Our purposes here are to help parents understand the real risks of teen driving, point out and counteract attitudes and assumptions that mislead parents, and empower parents to evaluate the circumstances of each day and say no when necessary. We want to give parents the benefit of the years of homework we have done, to spare families and communities the agony that results from preventable crashes, injuries, and fatalities.

Why do so many manuals and articles neglect predriving supervision? We live in a car-glorifying and auto-dependent society in which getting behind the wheel is prelude to freedom and adventure, not preparation for risk. Popular movies glorify car chases and sometimes even crashes. (One advertisement for high-definition television actually boasted that "cars smashing into little pieces look better in HD.") We hardly blink at the number of people—more than thirty-five thousand—who die on American roads every year. Traffic deaths are local news, the price of our mobile society. This is the cultural backdrop for parents when their teens reach the minimum driving age and step into a grown-up world of excitement and exploration.

Parents who are soon to face or are now immersed in this challenge, who pick up this book out of concern for their teen's safety, should understand the thankless task ahead. A parent who says no or "Not so fast!" to an eager teen driver is swimming against the tide. Parenting is hard and directing teens is harder, but keeping a teen driver safe may be a parent's greatest challenge. It requires, among other things, resisting pressure from both the teen's and parent's peers, counteracting an unrelenting barrage of advertising and media, inconveniencing ourselves, and recognizing the omissions, unconscious attitudes, and biases in what we read. Parents who take this book's advice—supervision first, driving second—will likely never be praised by their teens or others for saving lives or preventing injuries. They will need to be satisfied with the knowledge that they, well, went the extra mile.

Yet however daunting it may be to widen our focus when it comes to teen drivers, it is imperative that we try, because the consequences of a mistake behind the wheel are injury or death, not only to a family member but also to others—passengers, other drivers, pedestrians, and bystanders. Despite the gains that have been made in teen driver safety, car crashes remain the leading cause of death for fifteen- to twenty-year-olds. American teens are three times more likely than adult drivers to be involved in a fatal crash. In 2015, teens were involved in 9 percent of all fatal crashes on US roadways, despite accounting for just 6 percent of all licensed drivers. Their crashes claimed 4,702 lives. Forty percent of those fatalities were the teen driver, while the other 60 percent were their passengers, occupants of other vehicles, pedestrians, and bicyclists. No parent ever expects to bury her child, but an average of five teens die every day in car crashes. And as noted, in 2015, the number of families who experienced this preventable tragedy went up for the second consecutive year.

Crashes, injuries, and fatalities know no favorites; while it is true that teen boys crash more than teen girls, crashes occur in urban, suburban, and rural communities; in affluent, middle-class, and low-income households; across ethnicities and nationalities; and to well-behaved and mature teens as well as daredevils. A compilation of news headlines covering just a few weeks in 2016 illustrates the geographic scope:

Denver, Colorado: TEEN DRIVER KILLS PEDESTRIAN

Sullivan County, Michigan: TEN-YEAR-OLD SISTER OF EIGHTEEN-YEAR-OLD DRIVER DIES IN CRASH

Houston, Texas: TEEN DRIVER'S ARM ALMOST SEVERED IN CRASH

High Point, North Carolina: FIFTEEN-YEAR-OLD DRIVER'S FOURTEEN-YEAR-OLD PASSENGER DIES IN CRASH

Olney, Maryland: TEEN DRIVER'S ALCOHOL-RELATED CRASH KILLS PASSENGER

Culver City, California: FATHER KILLED AS TEEN DRIVER TRIES TO EVADE POLICE

Milwaukee, Wisconsin: SEVENTEEN-YEAR-OLD DRIVER'S CRASH KILLS TWO RELATIVES

Battle Ground, Washington: TEEN DRIVER DIES IN HEAD-ON COLLISION

Batavia, Illinois: FIFTEEN-YEAR-OLD DRIVER HITS, KILLS MOTORCYCLIST

Fall River, Massachusetts: TEEN DRIVING TO PROM KILLED IN ROLLOVER CRASH

Can parents ignore this book and still have their teens survive injury-free into adulthood? Certainly. Hundreds of thousands of teens do. The issue is whether parents wish to roll the dice or take steps to push the odds in their favor.

Supervision before driving is every bit as important to improving the odds and lowering crash rates as teaching teens how to turn at a busy intersection. There are many steps parents can take that are rarely covered in the available resources. If we can better educate the thousands of parents of teens who obtain a driver's license every year to consider handling a vehicle as step two, to stop their overexcited teens at the door with the words "Not so fast!" and to take steps to avoid dangers and traps, we can further reduce teen driver crashes, injuries, and deaths, and their incalculable impact on families and communities.

1

Tim's Story

During 2006, I was a regular, mainstream parent of a teen driver. I occasionally worried about my son's safety, but I was generally confident that the training I had given him—what state law required and the literature suggested—was sufficient.

On December 2, 2006, everything changed. My seventeen-year-old son Reid died in a one-car crash. Driving on a three-lane interstate highway that he probably had never driven before, on a dark night just after rain had stopped, and apparently traveling above the speed limit, he went too far into a curve before turning, then overcorrected and went into a spin. While the physics of the moment could have resulted in any number of trajectories, his car hit the point of a guardrail precisely at the middle of the driver's-side door, which crushed the left side of his chest. Had the impact occurred eighteen inches forward or backward, he would have survived. No alcohol, no drugs, no cell phone; his passengers were legal, and he was well within the state's curfew for teen drivers.

He died from speed, an unfamiliar road, and inexperience with how to handle a skid. His two passengers were injured and briefly hospitalized.

Reid's crash was a precursor to a string of horrific crashes in Connecticut. In August 2007, four teens died in one crash, and then in October, a seventeen-year-old driver killed himself, his fourteen-year-old sister, and her fifteen-year-old friend.

Reading news accounts of these other crashes, I reflected more intently on how I had—or hadn't—controlled Reid's driving. These tragedies focused me and indeed our entire state on the dangers of teen driving. I found myself alternately defending my own conduct but then asking—well, if I did what I was supposed to, why was Reid dead?

Comparing other crashes to Reid's, and other parents' actions to my own, allowed me to indulge the thought that I had been a responsible parent. Reid's mom and I had allowed him to buy a safe, sensible Volvo, not a race car. I had educated myself about Connecticut's teen driving laws, made sure Reid understood them, given him more than the required twenty hours of on-the-road instruction, enrolled him in a driving school, demanded that he always wear his seat belt, revoked his driving privileges when he had disobeyed our household's rules, and even twice confiscated his car for a week or more. He drove crash free for eleven months. Looking back, it did not seem that I had made some horrible, obvious mistake. So where did I go wrong? Would a stricter father's son still be alive?

Just a week before the first anniversary of Reid's crash, I was driving to work, listening to the morning radio news, when the announcer said that our governor was forming a Teen Safe Driving Task Force to revise Connecticut's laws, with the hope of reducing the recurring carnage on our roads. The report stated that bereaved parents would be among those asked to serve on the task force. When I got to my office, I called my state senator, my state representative, a friend who knew the commissioner of motor vehicles, and a colleague who knew the governor, and asked for their help in being appointed, which I was, a week later.

Our assignment was to review the state's teen driving laws. As we proceeded, I relived how I had trained Reid and how and when I had controlled his driving. I learned new facts about teen driving and discovered that while supervising my son, I had not been as well-informed a parent as I had thought.

In the late 1990s, Connecticut joined a growing list of states that adopted what are called graduated driver licensing (GDL) laws. New drivers—generally between ages fifteen and eighteen—face a prescribed classroom curriculum and a certain number of required driving hours supervised by an instructor, parent, or guardian. After the learner's permit stage, GDL rules delay new drivers from carrying passengers, usually for several months, and impose a curfew in the range of 9:00 PM to 1:00 AM. At eighteen, these drivers graduate to an unrestricted adult license. Beyond these basics, however, the state laws vary widely.

I learned that Connecticut in 2005–2006 had one of the nation's more lenient laws, allowing teens to obtain a license as early as four months after turning sixteen and with just twenty hours on the road and several hours of classroom instruction about speeding and drunk driving. For the first three months of being licensed, Connecticut teens could carry as passengers only a supervising driver and immediate family, but after that, they could pile their friends into their cars. The statewide curfew was midnight.

As I dug into the mountain of information made available to task force members, I remembered what I had been thinking when I let Reid drive. Reid's close friend Mike was a few months older, and his buddy Tom was a full year ahead; by early 2006, they both had licenses and cars. In January, Reid had completed his learner's permit training and received his license. In lockstep with just about every other parent in our suburban town, my wife and I had agreed to consider letting Reid buy a used car.

I'd taken him out on lightly traveled back roads. I'd reviewed the state's recommended list of skills and situations to be taught to new drivers, and we'd spent time on each one. We'd practiced evasive maneuvers in an empty parking lot early on a Sunday morning. While taking driver's ed, Reid had shown himself to me to be an alert, coordinated driver.

That our state had adopted GDL requirements was comforting. I'd assumed that the legislature, the Department of Motor Vehicles, and the police had gotten together to formulate sensible rules that, if followed, would keep Reid safe.

Finally, I cannot deny—nor, I think, can any busy parent—that having my son drive was alluringly convenient, living as we did in a suburban community in which walking was usually not an option. Reid getting his license provided an extra pickup and delivery service.

My wife and I overlaid our own rules onto state law. We were to know his destinations and his whereabouts at all times. Like all of his friends, he had a cell phone, and he was under orders to check in. We made it clear repeatedly that driving was a privilege and not a right. Our rules could be modified as needed based on particular circumstances, such as our judgment that he had not gotten enough sleep. Reid understood that when he arrived home I would be waiting for him and would conduct my own interrogation, checking for coherence and sobriety. On a few occasions when he missed his curfew, I confiscated his keys. Although I don't recall discussing it overtly with Reid, I think he also understood that I was regularly inspecting every nook and crevice in his car—just like his room—and I was keeping an eye on his mileage.

As I let the reins out on Reid's driving—longer periods in the car by himself, longer distances, driving at night or in bad weather—I relived my own driving experience and wondered if I had inadvertently conveyed any bad habits to my son. To my relief, he continued to show himself to be a calm, coordinated driver, with a good sense of the vehicle's position on the road. No news became good news.

In April, when Reid had been licensed for three months, an officer pulled him over for a moving violation: crossing two lanes without signaling. According to Reid, the violation was questionable. The fine was $204, which Reid paid from his own savings account.

As the summer wore on, I became concerned about Reid revving the engine—it was the only way he could make his clunky used car seem cool. I was not particularly alarmed but more concerned that he would rev the engine while on the road into an excessive speed and find himself with another expensive ticket. In late September, he was cited for driving 42 mph in a 25 mph zone. Because this was his second moving violation before turning eighteen, he not only incurred a fine but also had to attend a driver retraining class at the Department of Motor Vehicles. He signed up for the last possible day: December 2.

I suppose that subconsciously I appreciated that teenage drivers are inexperienced and not yet mentally mature. Yet I did not personally know any family that had lost a teenage driver in a crash; I had survived my own teen years; I knew my son—and had trained him—and I assumed that the state's laws would keep him safe.

But that's not what happened; Reid died six hours before he was due to attend the DMV retraining.

In my first two months serving on the task force, I sifted through a mountain of statistics, analyses, and reports and found that teen driving is more dangerous than I had understood while parenting Reid, and that Connecticut's GDL laws were weaker than I had realized. I had allowed Reid to drive in situations that were much more perilous than I had thought.

In addition to research, subcommittee meetings, and task force sessions, I met and spoke at length with police, psychologists, doctors, nurses, prosecutors, judges, school principals, driving instructors, social workers, traffic safety officials, and other bereaved parents. As I began to read and listen to facts and proposals for improving the laws, a question popped into my head and then repeated itself week after week, each time a bit louder and more tinged with disbelief: *Why had I not learned all of this earlier?* This was a maddening combination of outward questioning (*Why didn't anyone tell me?*) and inward (*Why didn't I better educate myself?*). Why had I not been more conservative in my decisions about Reid's driving? Like so many other parents, had I been seduced by the convenience of having another driver in the house?

During the first six months of 2008, the task force became nearly an obsession. We traveled to high schools across the state and appeared on statewide television. I was interviewed on WCBS radio about my reeducation.

Within four months—a quickness rare in the world of public policy—the task force recommended, the governor endorsed, and the legislature adopted stricter rules for sixteen- and seventeen-year-olds: doubling the required hours during the learner's permit stage; moving the curfew from midnight to 11:00 PM; prohibiting teen drivers from transporting anyone other than parents, guardians, and siblings until licensed for a full year; suspending licenses, starting at thirty days, for moving violations (instead of just monetary fines); providing faster court prosecutions and driver retraining sessions; requiring a parent or guardian to attend a two-hour safety class with each teen during driver's ed; requiring all passengers of teen drivers to wear seat belts; and allowing law enforcement to confiscate a teen's license and impound the car for forty-eight hours if the situation warranted.

After the governor signed the bill before a bank of TV cameras and a crowd of legislators in the sun-splashed courtyard of a high school, I calculated the difference these new laws would have made in the life of my son. Had the 2008 law been in effect in 2006, Reid would have had double the hours of required on-the-road training; my wife or I would have attended a safety class with him while he had his learner's permit; his first moving violation (the double lane change) would have earned him a thirty-day license suspension; his second violation would have cost him his license for sixty days, plus a fine for license reinstatement; he would have taken his driver retraining class sooner; and he would not have been allowed to have the passengers who were with him when he crashed. The new laws were too late but not too little.

When all of this settled in my mind, there was no doubt that I had to find a way to communicate my new perspectives to other parents. It was undeniably true that I had not fully appreciated how dangerous teen driving is in the best of circumstances or how risk escalates in a variety of predictable and therefore controllable situations. Having read all of the available literature and consulted the mainstream sources, I started to think that parents need better information.

And so, in October 2009, I started speaking out, by launching *From Reid's Dad*, my national blog for parents of teen drivers. Eighteen months and fifty posts later, I had the basis for what became the first edition of this book, published in 2013.

As soon as the first edition was published, it became clear that it fulfilled a need. *Publisher's Weekly* called it "a clear, concise, and potentially life-saving book that should be required reading for every parent before their teen gets behind the wheel." Allan Williams, a preeminent traffic safety researcher and formerly the chief scientist of the Insurance Institute for Highway Safety, lauded its evidence-based compilation of lessons. *Library Journal* called it "a welcome addition to an underserved topic." Teen safe driving advocates, traffic and youth safety organizations, and government agencies embraced its parent-role message as a complement to motor vehicle and rules-of-the-road instruction. The Governors Highway Safety Association, composed of the Highway Safety Offices of all fifty states and US territories, and the National Safety Council recognized the book with national public service awards.

The success of *Not So Fast*'s first edition prompted discussion of a second edition that would sharpen and improve the book's lessons, incorporate 2012–2016 research about teen driver safety, and update specifics. Yet as I contemplated a revision, it occurred to me that the book would benefit from an additional voice, a traffic safety expert, a highly regarded professional, and, if I could find such a person, a mother of a teen driver. My inquiries among what I now call my "traffic safety friends" yielded an immediate consensus about the most qualified person in the entire country to enlist as coauthor: Pam Shadel Fischer.

So, in 2016, I asked and she accepted. As we began our collaboration, it became immediately apparent that Pam would bring to this second edition not only the perspective of Zach's mom in addition to Reid's dad but also a depth and breadth of understanding of safe teen driving, honed from more than three decades of immersion in safer teen driving.

I am grateful for Pam's collaboration, but I am also elated for parents and readers who will now reap the benefits of her contributions.

2

Pam's Story

I've been a transportation safety consultant for thirty years, with a particular passion for teen driving. I successfully lobbied in my state for stronger teen licensing laws, chaired a highly respected commission that called for adoption of the nation's first novice driver decal requirement (a sticker that identifies to law enforcement when a teen is behind the wheel), and organized and built a successful statewide teen safe driving coalition. I also facilitated the nation's first all-teen safe driving commission, authored national best-practice reports, presented at dozens of state and national conferences, and gave more press interviews than I could count.

But being a mother to Zachary, my one and only child, has always been my most important transportation safety job.

I had been working for AAA for nearly a decade when Zach was born, so I leveraged my expertise to keep him safe. He rode, properly secured, in a child safety seat and then a booster seat until he was big enough to sit safely in a seat belt. He always wore a helmet when Rollerblading and ice skating, even when he was just in the driveway or at a nearby pond. I taught him to cross the street only at corners, never in between. My concern for his safety extended to the littlest of things—making sure his shoes were tied tightly, making him wear a hat on sunny days, cutting up his food to prevent a choking hazard. Sure, Zach got his share of bumps and bruises, and even a mad dash to the emergency room when I, unbeknownst to me, fed him a spoiled grilled cheese sandwich. (Five hours and lots of fluids later, he was fine.)

Yet when he turned sixteen, the minimum age for obtaining a learner's permit in my state, I began shaking in my boots, literally.

"You've got this—you're the safety mom," said all my friends. Certainly I knew all about the risks for teens. I could cite from memory the latest teen driver research findings. I understood how and why graduated driver licensing (GDL) works, and I had even taught a teen safe driving orientation program for parents. Still, that didn't change the fact that Zach, a smart, sensible, athletic kid, suffered from the same problems as every other teen driver: a lack of experience and an immature brain.

I was grateful that I had done my homework and purchased a vehicle with plenty of safety features, including front and side-impact airbags and traction stability control. I also took solace in the fact that I was an involved parent who gave her teen enough structured support to allow him to make good choices, while not compromising on safety. We even signed a parent-teen driving agreement.

Even so, my son still crashed—twice in nine days!

When the shock of those crashes wore off, the question arose: What could I learn from them? Without a doubt, I recognized that the first crash was the result of Zach's inexperience. As for the second, it was essentially a timing issue; if he had only left five minutes earlier or later, he would not have encountered the other driver whose lane crossing led to the crash. I reaffirmed to myself that by being an authoritative parent I was lowering his crash risk. In both crashes, he wasn't speeding or on his cell phone or impaired, and he and his passenger were buckled up—all behaviors reflective of teens who have parents who set and monitor safety rules.

We had practiced—a lot. Zach worked with a professional driving instructor, and I better educated myself about how to coach a new, young driver. (Yes, I knew plenty about teen driving, but I had never taught anyone to drive and didn't profess to know how to do it.)

Every time Zach and I got in the car, he took the wheel. For twelve months, he drove us to and from school, to ice hockey practice and games, to the grocery store and the mall, and to countless other places. Our travels prompted numerous teachable moments, ranging from getting out of the way of tailgaters and texters, to moving over for emergency vehicles, to using headlights in the rain. These scenarios helped him develop greater awareness of what to expect and how to react. We also practiced in all kinds of weather and on all types of roads. Since I was determined to expose him to as many driving scenarios as possible while I was still in the passenger seat, we kept a log of every trip.

Yet several months after Zach obtained his probationary or restricted license, and eighteen months after he first climbed into the driver's seat, he was involved in his first crash. "Mom, we've got a problem" were the four words I didn't want to hear when I picked up the phone. He had collided with a dump truck. Thankfully no one was hurt, but my car sustained $10,000 in damage.

Just nine days later, Zach called again, and this time his words were even more unsettling. "Mom, it's really bad," he said. "Where are you?" I asked. "Just up the street," he said. "I had no place to go; she hit me head-on." I don't remember putting on my boots or grabbing my coat; I just flew out the door and ran down the middle of the road. Zach and his passenger, a neighbor and high school hockey teammate, were being checked out by an EMT when I arrived. They, along with the driver of the other vehicle, also a teen, were not seriously injured, but the car Zach had been driving was a total loss.

While I was inclined to encase my son in bubble wrap and lock him in his room after this second crash, I knew that wasn't the answer. The only way he was going to become a better driver was to keep driving. So three days later, he was back on the road. I held my breath until he got safely to his destination and exhaled only after receiving his usual pithy text: "Here."

Zach and I discussed both crashes, which occurred just before Christmas, numerous times. The crashes turned out to be teachable events. Zach came to realize that in the first crash he had misjudged the distance and speed of the oncoming vehicle, a common cause of teen driver collisions. "I honestly thought I had enough time to make the turn," he said, "but I didn't know how fast he was going or how close he really was."

We talked through what he could and should have done, including using extreme caution when making a left turn (one of the most difficult maneuvers for all drivers, but especially teens), looking for large gaps in traffic, and being mindful of that message on the side-view mirror that reads, "Vehicles are closer than they appear." Most importantly, I stressed, "If you're not sure, don't go." We also talked about the fact that when cross-traffic was heavy, he could go straight or turn right and take a longer route.

The second crash was more difficult to analyze, because the other driver had failed to maintain her lane and crossed into oncoming traffic. Zach recounted that he was looking ahead (scanning the road is critical for safe driving, but it's not something new drivers do very well) and saw her sliding. "I slowed down and stopped," he said, "but I really didn't have anywhere to go. It was either steer away from her into this big tree or sit tight." He chose the latter—and learned how cars respond in frontal crashes.

That was another important takeaway from this second crash. Zach had heard me preach over and over the importance of buckling up. Both he and his passenger were wearing their seat belts, ensuring they were in the right position when the airbags deployed during the head-on collision. Additionally, there were two impacts: the oncoming vehicle hit Zach's car and then spun and hit him again on the driver-side passenger door. The car absorbed the forces of the crash, the passenger compartment remained intact, and Zach and his teammate, secured in their seat belts, remained inside that steel cocoon.

Since those crashes, I've never lost sight of the fact that Zach is gaining experience every time he gets behind the wheel, but he's not a safe driver yet. While he has been driving for six years and has been exposed to a myriad of driving situations, his brain is still developing, and it will be another couple of years, until he reaches his midtwenties, before his brain fully processes and recognizes risk. That's why I've stayed involved and will continue to do so.

I blogged about Zach's novice driving experience. (Let's just say he wasn't thrilled to be the subject of my musings.) While he was learning to drive, and after his crashes, I facilitated many parent-teen driving programs and shared my Safety Mom story. One message I shared was this:

I've only got one child, and he is not disposable. I did everything in my power—and that money can buy—to nurture, clothe, feed, inoculate, educate, and protect him for the first sixteen years of his life. So when he turned seventeen and obtained his driver's license, I was determined to do everything possible to ensure that my son would survive his most dangerous driving years. I wanted a return on my investment, and to see my son achieve a lifetime of milestones. Don't you want the same thing for your son or daughter?

Some parents I've encountered through my work in teen driving believe that teen driver crashes and the resulting injuries and fatalities are inevitable or a kind of teenage rite of passage. But having met far too many parents who have buried a teen as a result of a car crash, I can't and won't accept that. Teens will drive, but parents can and must protect them with informed, authoritative, daily, and loving supervision. It's my hope that after you read this book, you'll understand how to do so.

3

Why There Is No Such Thing as a Safe Teen Driver

In addition to teens who eagerly approach the age at which their state allows them to obtain a learner's permit and then a license, some teens receive encouragement—from friends, older siblings, and sometimes parents—to "get your license early," because it will extend their boundaries as a person, provide freedom to explore, and expand options for education and employment.

It's hard to argue with such advice. Getting a driver's license is a major step from childhood to young adulthood. Having a license allows teens to travel to school and extracurricular activities or a job, explore new places, broaden their knowledge of geography, and gain new perspectives on where and how people live and work.

So, with all these allures and benefits embedded in a teen getting a driver's license as soon as possible, why does advising teens to "get licensed early" make us shudder?

23

Because, unfortunately, *there is no such thing as a safe teen driver.* While getting a license "early" creates opportunities, it also elevates the risk of a disabling or fatal crash.

Why are all teens, including the levelheaded, risk-aware, and well-trained ones, at risk? There are four reasons:

- The human brain does not fully develop until we reach our early or midtwenties, and the last part of the brain to mature is the prefrontal cortex, the part that provides judgment and restraint and counterbalances the already developed part that creates desire, excitement, and risk-taking.
- Driving requires the continuous evaluation of hundreds of ever-changing factors and circumstances, and thus experts say that it takes three to five *years* of experience to become familiar and comfortable with the myriad situations that drivers encounter, not the twenty to one hundred *hours* that most states require for a teen to obtain a license.
- New drivers generally look at the perimeter of their car and focus on not hitting anything, rather than looking down the road (or scanning the driving environment), where they would see developing situations and dangers.
- We train teens on local, familiar roads, but driving inevitably takes them to highways and unfamiliar places, so they must learn to drive while also trying to navigate.

Thus teen drivers, no matter how well intentioned, trustworthy, respectful, schooled in safe driving laws, and thoroughly trained in how to safely operate a car, *do not have and cannot obtain* the essential elements of a safe driver: a brain that quickly and accurately perceives and responds to danger; judgment to deal with a variety of fast-moving and ever-changing situations that every driver faces; confidence to look ahead down the road instead of focusing on the car's perimeter; experience to concentrate on what the car's next maneuvers will be instead of how to execute them; and enough time behind the wheel so that most driving will be with a familiar vehicle on a familiar road. Developing these characteristics takes considerable time, which cannot be cut short or accelerated.

The slow-to-mature brain is the most problematic factor; the teen brain is simply constrained physically and chemically. The prefrontal cortex—which provides the connectivity (a.k.a., wiring) that enables organization, planning, interpretation, and inhibition—is the last part of the brain to develop, typically being complete around age twenty-five. But the lobe that generates emotion is in place years earlier, thus accounting for teens' penchant for reacting more from emotion than reason.

This phenomenon also results from the brain's generation of chemicals known as neurotransmitters. One chemical, called dopamine, stimulates the desire for excitement, and another, serotonin, alerts the body to risk and prompts defensive actions. In a teen brain, dopamine outweighs serotonin. As one doctor explains it, dopamine is the gas and serotonin is the brakes, so teens are mentally more gas than brake.

Applied to driving, these twin realities mean that teen drivers do not recognize hazards or assess the risks in a complex traffic situation, and so their reactions are often late and their decisions poor. Only the completion of the brain's physical development and the resulting balanced chemical proportions can overcome this barrier to safe driving.

It is important to note that *safe* is a relative term. All driving is risky. Drivers aged thirty-five to forty-nine have the lowest crash rates. Their brains are fully developed, their combination of experience and good reflexes is the best of any driver group, and they have the greatest personal and professional reasons to drive safely. Yet middle-aged drivers are *safer*, not safe. Teen drivers are at significantly *greater* risk.

So yes, a driver's license can help a teen with school, a job, and knowledge of the world. But these enticements should not distract or blind us from the fact that the risks of teen driving are substantial and largely unchangeable except through years of physical growth, emotional maturity, and much more experience than state licensing laws typically require.

4

Baseline Dangers
and Higher-Risk Factors

John Rosemond, the parenting advice columnist, once posed this question to parents of teens: "Would you allow your son or daughter to participate in an activity that had a one in 10,000 chance of death?" Not surprisingly, his readers said no.

Then Rosemond revealed that the activity he was talking about was driving.

The government, insurance companies, and highway safety analysts and advocates have collected mountains of data about driving. The numbers they report vary somewhat, but in round numbers there are today approximately 11.7 million teen drivers (ages fifteen to twenty) in the United States (a 7 percent drop since 2005), and during the decade 2005–2014, an average of 2,279 teen drivers died and another 180,000 were injured *annually* in crashes.

These numbers hide the fact that even the best-trained, most law-abiding teens are at risk, and there are several behaviors while driving that elevate the risk far above these scary-enough-as-is averages.

Teen driving always involves what experts call baseline dangers. As noted earlier, the teenage brain does not yet fully appreciate risks, and teens lack the experience and judgment essential to driving. Safe driving takes years, and new drivers are learning simultaneously to drive, navigate, and extend their vision beyond the front of the car. Studies consistently show that teen drivers most often crash due to inattention to traffic conditions, speeding, following too closely, and not yielding to other vehicles when turning. Thus, if we prepared a safety scale for teen drivers and assigned a label to each tier, the lowest, safest level would be "at risk," not "safe."

The point is that for teens, the dangers start at "at risk" and go up from there. It is impossible to rank these risk-elevating factors or assign them point totals, because each factor has its own variations and levels—speed and blood alcohol level, for example. We do have approximations, however, such as the study's conclusion that drivers (of any age) who text are twenty-three times more likely to crash than those who don't. Here are factors that spike the punchbowl, so to speak:

- drugs, alcohol, lack of sleep, and anything that impairs reflexes and judgment
- distracted driving (texting, cell phones, iPods, other electronic devices)
- speeding
- passengers
- failure to use seat belts
- bad weather
- night driving

- impulsiveness and aggressive behavior
- attention deficit disorder or any similar cognitive condition

These factors make the averages discussed earlier virtually meaningless. For even the safest teen driver, these higher-risk factors push the odds of an average teen getting into a serious crash into the "waiting to happen" category. Then, if a teen driver combines one or more of these higher-risk factors, such as speeding and passengers with a cell phone and alcohol, the relevance of these averages diminishes even further, because the likelihood of a debilitating crash becomes even higher.

Teens with attention deficit disorder (ADD) and attention deficit hyperactivity disorder (ADHD) require an additional level of supervision. Distractibility, an inability to focus for lengthy time periods, and an elevated tendency to take risks are, of course, at odds with safe driving. Many teens can control ADD/ADHD behaviors with medication, and thus it is essential that teens with these conditions take the proper dosage before driving. Some teens with more severe symptoms, however, simply should not drive at all. If you're the parent of a teen who has been diagnosed with either of these conditions, consult with his or her doctor to discuss proper dosage for driving and whether your teen's symptoms are severe enough to warrant a total or partial ban on driving.

To bring the point back to Rosemond: bear in mind and explain to your teens that the likelihood of them getting into a serious crash is high to begin with but that there are behaviors that elevate that risk to near certainty.

The baseline dangers also have a time-of-year element: teen crashes increase 16 percent during the four summer months, which traffic safety officials and advocates call "the 100 deadliest days." The statistics are sobering:

- From 2010 to 2015, more than five thousand people died in crashes involving teen drivers, meaning that on average, one thousand people died between Memorial Day and Labor Day each year.
- Nine out of the ten deadliest days for teens fall between May and August, with July 4 being the most dangerous.

Figuring out why there are more fatalities in the summer months is not difficult. It is due to the difference between purposeful and recreational driving, discussed in chapter 11. When teens have a destination, a route, a timetable, and a consequence for not arriving on time, they are far more likely to arrive safely than when they are joyriding—that is, driving for fun. Why does joyriding increase substantially during the late spring and summer months? Proms, and trips to the beach, the mall, the movies, and concerts are all joyriding, in the sense that there is no consequence for being late.

This book describes steps that parents need to take to minimize risks for their teen drivers year-round, but especially from May through August.

"My Kid Is Very Responsible!"

As the statewide task force on which Tim served began to consider stricter teen licensing requirements in early 2008, e-mails from parents began arriving at a website set up by the Department of Motor Vehicles. While many parents expressed support for stricter laws, some were opposed, and some were outraged (a response encountered by government officials in many states). They raised objections, such as:

- I don't want to see my children punished with severe restrictions just because they are teenagers.
- It should be a parent's choice if they want their new driver to be in the car with another person. Another person makes the new driver better because they are another set of eyes.
- While the intention is to reduce the incidence of horrific accidents that maim or kill multiple teens, the fact is that

teens need to rely on each other for transportation, and
these laws would cause a huge inconvenience.

- If teens cannot carry passengers then they are forced to
drive alone, which wastes gas and money and puts more
cars on the road, which is bad for air quality.
- Teenagers have very busy lives.
- The fact is that our children have to grow up, and to
do that they have to make mistakes, and some of those
mistakes will be fatal.

Ironically, these e-mails helped convince task force members
that Connecticut needed a stronger law.

In 2012, a parent wrote to a newspaper's opinion page about
American teen driving laws: If our country were as small as most
European countries, making kids wait until they're 18 to get
their licenses might be more reasonable. Europe has better mass
transit. But to expect parents to drive their little darlings to and
from school, to and from work, and to and from all social activities is not reasonable.

Do you agree? Does this parent's attitude sound similar to your
thought process? We hope not. The author did not appear to be
aware that if the minimum driving age were based on the science
of brain development rather than tradition and political pushback
from parents, the starting age would be in the range of twenty-
one to twenty-five, not sixteen to eighteen. This writer also placed
convenience ahead of safety; the words signal an impatience with
teens not getting their licenses because of the imposition on parents' schedules. The implication is a willingness to force a teen who
may not be ready to drive to do so because "it's time to grow up."

Parental oversight can also be hindered by defensiveness. Some
consider their teen's driving a reflection of their attentiveness and

performance as a parent. Any suggestion that the teen is not a good driver constitutes a personal insult. The thought that our own teens are more responsible than others because we ourselves are responsible can get in the way of clear thinking about how best to control driving.

So how should parents approach their teen's driving? We can divide parent attitudes into dos and don'ts, starting with the latter:

- Don't let your personal convenience get in the way of safety.
- Don't be desensitized by popular culture, entertainment, and the news media to the dangers of driving.
- Don't be lulled into a false sense of security, believing that a responsible teen who has taken driver's ed and passed the state's road test is a safe driver.
- Don't be reckless or indifferent.

Instead, we recommend the following:

- Understand and accept the dangers of teen driving as the baseline.
- Appreciate the importance of professional driving instructors and support their work with your teen.
- Recognize that the end of driver's ed classes is the start of daily, heightened parental supervision and involvement.
- Realize that a newly licensed teen is a beginner taking on a dangerous task.
- Be willing to say no to your teens, especially at three stages: (1) when they want to get a learner's permit, but your heart and head tell you that they are not ready yet; (2) when they want to graduate from a learner's permit

to licensed solo driving, but you have the same fear; and (3) when your licensed driver, day by day, runs into circumstances, such as fatigue or stress, that prompt you to say, "No driving today."

- Use your parental power to withhold car keys when you need to, and don't try to curry favor with a teen by making keys available.
- Be vigilant day to day for the situations described in this book: purposeful driving versus joyriding, managing curfews, prohibiting passengers, prohibiting texting, not buying a car for a teen's own use, using a traffic ticket as a teachable moment, and signing and following a teen driving agreement.
- When in doubt, err on the side of being conservative. There is simply no room for error when we manage teen drivers.
- Approach parenting your teen driver with the attitude of working together to make safety the top priority.
- Never forget that teens need parents; they already have friends.

It may be useful to think of parenting teen drivers on a scale of worst to best: reckless, indifferent, ignorant; informed but not proactive; willing but misinformed; and informed and proactive. Strive to be in this last category, which research confirms cuts teens' crash risk and the likelihood of them engaging in unsafe driving behaviors such as texting, drinking, speeding, and not wearing a seat belt.

6

What Driver's Ed Is and Isn't

W hen we refer to driver's ed, we mean all types of teen driver training and education, whether provided by parents, guardians, relatives, other adult supervising drivers, high schools, or commercial driving schools.

Depending on what state you live in, teens may or may not have to complete a formal driver education and training program, which typically consists of classroom and behind-the-wheel instruction. Currently, less than half of the states require the youngest teen drivers (typically under eighteen) to take driver's ed, and only a few require teens to complete a prelicensing drug and alcohol awareness program. Parents should consult their state's licensing agency website for specifics on what their teen must do.

But does driver's ed work? The general consensus until a few years ago was no (which explains the decline in state funding for driver education and the elimination of such programs from many public schools). Recent research, however, suggests that driver education is a worthy expenditure and one that states should consider for all novice teen drivers—even those teens who wait until age eighteen or nineteen to obtain a license. While parents may not want to pay someone else to teach their teen how to drive (costs range from several hundred dollars to thousands), *teens who complete formal driver's ed have fewer crashes and lower violation, conviction, and suspension rates than teens who don't.*

As already noted, however, completion of driver's ed does not mean that a teen is a safe driver. In fact, it's only the first step of a beginner who is undertaking a dangerous activity. (Pam has lost count of the number of parents who have said to her, "I paid my teen's driving instructor $350 for six hours of lessons, and he isn't a good driver.") Yes, professional instruction can help teens learn the rules of the road, the basics of safe vehicle operation, and how to pass the state's written and road skills tests. Moreover, without question, the more hours teens spend behind the wheel receiving supervised training, the better drivers they will be when they begin driving solo.

The primary problem is that driver's ed, which typically provides thirty to forty-five hours of classroom lectures and six to twenty hours on the road, does not and cannot overcome the reasons why there is no such thing as a safe teen driver (see chapter 3). Driver's ed is necessary and can help, but it is not sufficient to overcome the immaturity of the teen brain or provide enough experience to create a safe, skilled driver. (One public policy consequence of this reality is that state laws that allow earlier licensing for teens who take a driver education course mislead parents into thinking that graduates of driver's ed are safe drivers who no longer need continual supervision.)

In other words, when a teen is taking a driver's ed course, and after a teen finishes this formal instruction, parents must step up and into the roles of driving coach and supervisor. This can be a daunting task; many parents believe they aren't equipped to teach their teen to drive, and often consider this the scariest, most nerve-racking thing they have ever done.

What should parents do to help their teen develop driving skills? Start by taking advantage of free teen driving resources that are available from most state licensing agencies, insurance companies, and safety organizations. (See Teen Driving Resources, page 140.) These parent guides address critical skills such as merging and passing, scanning the road, and allowing adequate following distance, and keeping a practice driving log of when and where teens drive.

Second, talk to your teen's driver's ed instructor for tips on how best to train and coach your beginning driver. Even consider asking for in-car instruction where the parent assumes the role of the student driver and learns how the professional delivers instructions, guidance, and connections.

Finally, take the time after every practice driving session to talk to your teen about what he or she experienced on the road. Ask your teen to describe what was going on during driving (called commentary driving) and how his or her actions while on the road impacted safety. Use your teen's time on the road so that it becomes more than practice and results in a deeper discussion about decision making and the importance of staying focused on safety.

But let us return to the underlying reality: teens who have taken driver's ed, supplemented by practice with a parent, are still beginners at a dangerous activity and still held back by their brains not yet fully recognizing risk. Parents must remain involved with their teen driver during and after driver's ed.

Parents should not fear or shrink from this role; contrary to what parents may think, teens welcome our input, and most concede that Mom and Dad profoundly influence how they drive.

7

The ABCs of GDL
(Graduated Driver Licensing)

E very parent of a teen driver should understand the basics of graduated driver licensing (GDL), which is in place in some form in every state. The critical facts, proven by mountains of research, are that GDL targets the most frequent dangers of teen driving and imposes requirements that help to reduce them. It is also now fully established that the stricter a state's GDL law is, the lower the teen driver crash rate.

GDL is a three-stage licensing system that corresponds to a teen driver's age and experience, and includes: a supervised learner's permit phase, an unsupervised license phase with restrictions that address the primary causes of teen driver crashes, and finally a full license with all restrictions lifted. The components of GDL include:

- a specified minimum age at which a teen may obtain a learner's permit and then a restricted license (referred

to as a restricted, provisional, intermediate, junior, or probationary license)
- hours of on-the-road training that a learner's permit holder must receive from a driving instructor, parent, guardian, or supervising adult before obtaining a restricted license
- limits on passengers during the learner's permit and restricted license phases
- a curfew (evening/late night into the early morning) when teens may not be on the road
- rules about electronic devices and texting (which are often stricter than for older drivers)
- seat belt rules, such as requiring every passenger to buckle up when a teen is driving
- monetary fines, license suspensions, license revocations, or some combination for first-time and repeat offenders

A handful of state GDL laws also include a requirement that parents attend an educational program to learn about the risks for novice drivers, how and why GDL addresses that risk, and resources available to help them coach and monitor their teens.

Regardless of whether your state has such a requirement, it is critical for parents to learn about GDL and understand that it is a *parent program*, not a police program. GDL contains restrictions and requirements that parents must enforce. The importance of parents understanding and enforcing GDL cannot be overstated. GDL is not a suggestion or a guideline but a minimum standard for parent supervision.

It's also important to understand that each state establishes its own motor vehicle laws, including those addressing teen drivers. The federal government generally does not intrude on this state power, the exceptions being withholding federal funds for highway construction and maintenance to incentivize states to follow a minimum national driving standard, such as establishing twenty-one as the legal drinking age and making seat belts mandatory. Thus, at this time, although the federal government provides financial incentives for states to adopt a GDL law that meets specified minimum standards, there is no federal requirement that they do so. The other critical fact is that state GDL laws vary widely, with a few states having minimal rules and only a few featuring strict requirements throughout their statutes.

At minimum, a GDL law should:

- allow a learner's permit no earlier than age fifteen
- require that a learner's permit be held for at least six months before a teen applies for a restricted license
- require a minimum of fifty hours of supervised practice driving, with ten of those hours logged after dark
- provide for a restricted license phase that begins no earlier than age sixteen
- contain a night driving restriction that begins no later than 10:01 PM and ends no earlier than 5:59 AM
- restrict teen drivers to one or no passengers, including family members under twenty-one
- ban the use of handheld and hands-free electronic devices
- require that everyone in the vehicle be properly restrained in seat belts or car seats
- allow an unrestricted license no earlier than age eighteen

Put another way, GDL laws work because they take direct aim at the leading causes of teen driver crashes and fatalities: they delay the issuance of learner's permits and licenses, restrict passengers, require education about and ban impaired and distracted driving, keep teens off the road late at night and early in the morning, establish seat belt rules, and specify penalties for violations. GDL allows teens to gain on-the-road experience under less challenging conditions, such as supervised, daytime operation. Research shows that GDL systems are the most effective tool for addressing teen crash risk; when a state makes its GDL stricter, crash rates, injuries, and fatalities decline.

Several national organizations regularly track, compare, or rate state teen driver laws, such as the Governors Highway Safety Association (www.ghsa.org), the Insurance Institute for Highway Safety (www.iihs.org), and Advocates for Highway and Auto Safety (www.saferoads.org). State motor vehicle department websites explain each state's legal requirements. Parents should determine how strict their own state's GDL program is, because the stricter a state's law, the more help a parent has in controlling a teen driver, *but the more lenient a state's law, the more responsibility the parent has to impose rules over and above the state's.*

While some parents chafe under the inconvenience and obligations that GDL laws impose, we encourage parents to recognize that these laws are intended to shield them from having to negotiate with their teen about whether particular situations are safe. For example, if a teen says, "I'd like to drive with two friends to the movie theater, and we'll be home by 1:00 AM," a GDL law midnight curfew gives parents the ability to respond, "I would like to say yes, but I can't, because you would be violating the law."

In our collective experience, we have learned several realities about GDL laws. First, the most vocal opposition to stronger GDL programs comes from parents—those who view teen drivers through the lens of their own convenience, the misplaced attitude that their well-behaved teen will never crash, or the misguided notion that the way to help teens grow up is to let them drive. Second, political change for the most part occurs incrementally, with small changes in a given year being easier for legislators to approve. As a result, in states where the GDL requirements are well below the standards supported by research and specified in federal incentive programs, bringing teen driver laws up to prescribed standards will likely take years.

Finally (this will come as a shock), politicians react to news events. It often takes multiple-fatality crashes involving teen drivers to create a public outcry that induces elected officials to adopt stricter laws. Sadly, for those working to prevent crashes and save lives in their states, it takes a tragedy to get legislators to muster the political will to toughen teen driver laws. In addition, among legislators, "GDL fatigue" can set in; elected officials may think that once a GDL law has been enacted or recently revised, the state's teen driving worries have been solved or that the most recent change should be given time to see if it works.

Another impediment is the attitude that some progress in fatality rates is enough. There is no doubt that GDL has sparked the steady decline in teen driver crashes, injuries, and fatalities in states across the nation. But that decrease may be coming to an end, as evidenced by the 11 percent increase in fatal teen crashes from 2014 to 2015. This increase highlights that we must never lose sight of the facts: even one teen driver injury is too many, teen driving is inherently unsafe, and parents must take the lead in putting GDL to work for their teens.

8

When Should a Teen Start Driving?

S hould the minimum age for licensing teen drivers be fifteen, sixteen, seventeen, eighteen, or even higher? This issue has been debated for years by legislators and traffic safety professionals across the country. It's important to recognize, however, that the question itself can mislead parents.

When state governments adopt teen driving laws they establish minimums, what lawyers call bright-line standards, meaning that whether or not the rule is good public policy, at least it is clear. If the minimum age is sixteen, and your teen is fifteen years and 364 days old, he cannot get a learner's permit or a license, but if he is sixteen years and one day old, he can. Put another way, teen driver laws tell us when a teen becomes eligible to apply for a permit or a license; the teen's birth certificate does the rest.

Thus, when each state sets a minimum age for a learner's permit or license, it establishes a single rule for every teen and every family in that state. Most states allow teens to obtain learner's permits when they turn fifteen or sixteen (a few start at age fourteen), and a so-called restricted, provisional, or junior license anywhere from three, six, or nine months later. When raising the minimum age to seventeen or eighteen is considered, some argue that the increase would actually make it harder for parents to train their teens to drive, since so many teens leave the house around age eighteen, to attend college or to work. On the other hand, New Jersey has established a minimum restricted licensing age of seventeen and a minimum full licensing age of eighteen, which research confirms has significantly reduced crash and fatality rates while having no impact on licensure rates.

However, asking what the statewide minimum age should be is the wrong question. Instead, the proper question should be: At what age should *your* teen be allowed to drive, regardless of what state law says? Some commentators call this the age of responsibility to distinguish it from the age of eligibility.

Parents need to be aware that each state's minimum driving age is influenced by politics (legislators vying for support and parents' votes), tradition (the minimum age has been fifteen or sixteen for a generation), culture (America romanticizes its automobiles), and simplicity (governments need rules that are easy to administer). But in no way, shape, or form are minimum driving age laws based on science or traffic safety data that show some teens can safely drive at age sixteen, seventeen, or eighteen. In fact, these ages are directly *contrary* to what science, crash data, and numerous teen driver studies tell us that the minimum driving age should be: twenty-one or older.

So, parents, do not be misled: state law may say that your son or daughter is now old enough to drive, but in your judgment, is he or she truly ready to take on this awesome responsibility? Assess the following factors:

- Appreciation of risk: Is your teen a risk taker?
- Emotional maturity: Can your teen handle the stress of driving?
- Physical maturity: Is your teen coordinated enough to handle a car, strong enough to change a tire, etc.?
- Fear: Will the dangers of driving overwhelm your teen's driver training?

Every parent needs to answer these questions. Those who don't are sidestepping a crucial responsibility. At the same time, the two factors that should have no place whatsoever in your decision are the convenience of having another driver in the house and pressure from peers—yours or your teen's.

Just because your state's teen driver law allows your teen to obtain a license does not mean that the state has determined that age is safe; it is up to you to be the extra filter in the process. Only you can decide whether your teen is ready to learn to become a responsible driver. Forget the legal age and focus on the age of responsibility. Your state may have a law, *but you have a veto*.

There is one more complication to the minimum age issue: one in three teens is not licensed when they turn eighteen, a substantial drop from a decade ago. While press reports have suggested that strict licensing laws or teens' abilities to interact with friends via social media are the cause for this decline, the documented cause is economics. Numerous studies confirm that the economic downturn of 2007–2012 and increases in gas prices made the cost of owning and operating a vehicle a hardship for many families, with the result that teens delayed obtaining licenses.

This is problematic because in nearly every state, graduated driver licensing requirements end at age eighteen, despite the fact that eighteen- to twenty-five-year-olds are still high-risk drivers.

This also means that teens who wait until age eighteen or older to obtain a license do not obtain the benefits of GDL; in effect, they go from zero to sixty without stops and restrictions.

But parents of teens who start driving after they have aged out of GDL can still impose a GDL-type plan, which should include:

- preparing your teen as if he or she is getting a learner's permit by reading up on your state's motor vehicle laws and the stages of GDL
- obtaining behind-the-wheel training from a professional through a state-approved driving school
- designating an experienced licensed adult driver to supervise your teen's beginning driving, until both the teen and the supervising driver determine that solo driving is appropriate
- gradually transitioning from supervised driving to independent driving under less risky situations, to driving in high-risk conditions
- enlisting an experienced adult to ride along as a passenger to provide guidance in complex driving situations

Determining when a teen is ready to obtain a learner's permit or a license is a parental *decision* that must be based on the factors described in this chapter and this book. A teen's birthday may prompt this decision-making process but should not control or preempt it.

9

Acting Like an
Air Traffic Controller

In 2011, the national media reported on air traffic controllers falling asleep on the job. Thinking of teen drivers as pilots and parents as air traffic controllers is actually not a bad analogy. Parents should treat every time their teen proposes to get behind the wheel as the equivalent of a pilot wanting to fly a plane. Teens should be required to file a flight plan and get permission from the tower—you—before taking off.

The elements of this flight plan should include what a pilot would consider essential:

- Destination: Where exactly are you going? (Pilots don't estimate—they need precision.)
- Route: What directions will get you there, and are there safety concerns associated with that course?
- Time of day: When are you leaving, and are there any safety issues implicit in your timetable (for example, night driving)?

- Equipment readiness: Do you have sufficient fuel, and is your equipment maintained and safe?
- Communications plan: When and how will you report your arrival at your destination, a problem or delay, and your departure time to return home?
- Passengers: Who will be with you, where will they sit, and how will you ensure that they don't distract you?
- Contingency plan: What will be your alternate route if the intended one is blocked or otherwise not available?
- Return trip: Do you have a set departure time, route, timetable, and passenger list (same considerations as the first leg of the trip)?
- Mental state: Are you well rested and alert?
- Overall: Are you ready to undertake this responsibility?

Only when each of these items has been satisfactorily planned should your teen be cleared for departure.

Sound silly? Overkill? If you think so, we respectfully suggest that you return to the dangers of teen driving. The risks of an unprepared pilot flying are not unlike those facing a teen driver. The margin for error is extremely small, and the risks are enormous.

A significant benefit of thinking of teen driving like a pilot's flight is that it should help you and your teen focus on the difference between driving with a destination, purpose, and timetable, and joyriding (more on this in chapter 11). Pilots don't joyride, in the sense that they don't fly a plane "just to go hang out with friends." Even when flying is recreational, a pilot prepares and files a plan.

Planning the route is especially important, for a pilot and for a teen. *New drivers should not be allowed to drive a route that a supervising adult does not know.* Supervising adults should consider whether there are locations on that route that are potentially unsafe, such as a curve at the end of a straightaway, a left-lane merge onto a busy highway, a stretch of three- or four-lane highway where drivers are constantly changing lanes to get to exits, places with poor visibility, unfamiliar roundabouts with multiple entry points, and so on. Parents should instruct teens to take a route that avoids these more dangerous places, or at least warn them what they will face in that location.

Texting is an easy way for your teen to report in, but with a clear understanding about pulling over and stopping in a safe place first. More than half of teens report receiving a text when they're driving from a parent asking them to *check in*, and feel pressured to respond right away since it came from Mom or Dad.

Will this air traffic controller routine feel a bit less necessary when your teen is on her one hundredth "flight" and has gotten the checklist down quite well? Yes. And will you need to maintain this level of detail after you and your teen have spent perhaps a year in this mode, taking every driving episode so seriously that each of the steps listed above becomes automatic? Probably not. There will come a time when it will not be as critical to be as deliberate and mechanical as suggested above. But the likelihood that your teen will get to this later stage is substantially increased if, as she begins to drive, you and she treat every situation as if she is a pilot preparing to fly a plane, and your supervision resembles that of a certified flight controller—one who is awake and on the job at all times.

This air traffic controller mode also raises a question: Should you use technology to track or monitor your teen driver? While teens may consider it an invasion of their privacy, many parents are taking advantage of an array of technologies to keep tabs on their teens' driving. Global positioning systems, or GPS-based vehicle monitoring options, for example, range from smartphone apps that alert parents when their teens are driving faster than a preset speed to devices that are either plugged in to the vehicle's diagnostic computer or professionally installed. *Research has found that teens drive differently in vehicles equipped with these devices, taking fewer risks behind the wheel.* Some insurance companies make monitoring devices (telematics) available to customers at no cost and provide discounts if they are permanently installed.

Geofencing—the use of GPS or local radio frequency identifiers (Wi-Fi or Bluetooth)—is another way to keep tabs on your teen driver. While early geofencing required expensive hardware and software, it is readily available today on smartphones. For parents' purposes, installing a geofencing app on a phone can help keep track of a teen's whereabouts. A variety of apps are available that make it simple to set up zones with corresponding notifications, such as "Jimmy arrived at school" or "Susie forgot to call when she arrived at work." Some apps feature maps that allow parents to check locations and set location-aware alerts.

We have also heard from parents who are using "find my phone" apps to monitor their teen driver's location. These apps enable parents who have access to their teen's cellular accounts to locate their teen's device on a map. Some apps will not only locate the phone on a map but also remotely lock it, play a sound, and display a message. For a parent worried about a teen who is late or has failed to arrive at a destination, this technology can provide peace of mind.

We suggest, however, that parents and teens have a conversation before installing any technology of this type. Not letting teens know they're being monitored will likely undermine trust and encourage defiant behavior if the "snooping" is eventually detected.

10

Negotiating and Enforcing a Parent-Teen Driving Agreement

Written agreements express terms and conditions in agreed-upon words, and signing our names to an agreement affirms our commitment to carry out the stated stipulations. We do this when buying or selling a home or business, starting a new job, performing a service such home renovations, and arranging countless other situations. Agreeing upon clear terms and complying with them allows us to define expectations, manage risks, reduce tensions, and create certainty and predictability.

Parental oversight of teen driving is one relationship that can be managed through a written agreement. In light of the risks of teen driving, parents need every tool available, and a good written agreement is one that traffic safety advocates can provide.

The problem is that there are hundreds of parent-teen driving agreements available to families. They vary widely in length, style, and provisions. Agreements are written, promoted, and distributed by government agencies, insurance companies, driving schools, cellular service providers, traffic safety organizations, hospitals, youth groups, personal injury attorneys, and many others. Many of these agreements are customizable, while some may only be used exactly as written. Topics covered sometimes range well beyond basic safe driving, to include such matters as financial cost allocation, grade-point averages, smoking, carrying firearms, performing household chores, respecting law enforcement, and picking up hitchhikers.

Therein lies the issue: there is such an array of agreements available to parents (who are presumably the ones most likely to search for one) that finding one that is user-friendly, well written, appropriately focused, customizable, and consistent with state law can be a difficult task. As a result, the few studies examining teen driving agreements conclude that while they can be a valuable safe driving tool, relatively few households negotiate, sign, and enforce one.

For simplicity, we will refer here to parent-teen driving agreements as PTDAs. PTDAs should aim for (1) striking the right balance between simplicity and complexity; (2) aligning prohibitions and requirements with the major causes of teen driver crashes; (3) ensuring consistency with state laws while allowing parents and teens to adopt stricter, customized rules; and (4) weeding out words, phrases, and provisions that can inadvertently confuse the situation or undercut the agreement and compliance.

One of the most important purposes of a PTDA is to allow parents and teens to establish rules for new teen drivers that *exceed a state's teen driving laws or fill gaps in a state's rules.* Although many individuals and organizations at both the state and federal levels are working to adopt stricter state teen driver laws, requirements still vary widely from state to state, ranging from one state's prohibition on driving before age seventeen to states that allow fourteen-year-olds to drive with few restrictions. By using a PTDA, families can establish standards that go beyond a state's lenient provisions and bring the rules for their household into better alignment with established teen driver safety research and best practices. In other words, *the weaker a state's teen driving laws, the greater the need for a good, customizable model PTDA.*

At a minimum, a PTDA is a written, signed agreement between a teen driver and his or her parent, guardian, or supervising adult that states rules for the teen driver's conduct for a defined time period and establishes what will happen if the teen violates those rules. A PTDA is not:

- a legally binding agreement that a parent/guardian or teen may enforce in court
- a substitute for on-the-road driver training
- a basis to allow a teen who is not yet ready to drive safely to get behind the wheel
- a reason for a parent, guardian, or supervising adult to be less vigilant about safety risks
- a defense against liability if a parent is sued

A PTDA is also not a *contract* but an *agreement*. It is intended to be not a treaty between adversaries but a consensus between partners. One primary purpose of a PTDA is to lead parents and teens to have discussions, before the teen starts driving, instead of after a crash or a ticket, about when and how permission to drive will be granted on a daily basis and what will happen in the event of a violation.

The keys to a strong agreement are mutually accepted statements about why an agreement is necessary, rules that can be followed without excessive difficulty or cost, and consensus about what will happen in the event of a violation. Additionally, to successfully direct and control conduct, PTDAs should be clearly written and easily understood, and focused on the conduct that the parties are concerned about—and nothing more. A strong PTDA will include the dangers of teen driving and the need for the agreement; provisions that remind all involved that parents retain ultimate responsibility and should act as role models for their teens; and the key factors affecting teen driver safety, including delayed brain development, speeding and reckless driving, alcohol and drug use, seat belts, electronic devices, and passengers.

Several situations and provisions can undercut any agreement's effectiveness, such as one party dictating all or most of the terms, using provisions that are so wordy or vague as to make the obligation unclear, using terms that are contrary to law, and stating provisions for which compliance is so difficult or costly as to give one party an incentive to violate the terms. As such, PTDAs must be negotiated, not dictated; easily understood; written so compliance with law is the minimum standard; and consistent within a family's circumstances and lifestyle.

All PTDAs should avoid the use of bare-bones wording (e.g., "I will drive safely at all times") that doesn't adequately explain the teen driving risks or rules that the agreement is trying to establish. Wordiness that tries to sound legal but instead causes confusion (e.g., "The party of the first part, hereinafter called the 'Teen Driver' . . .") should be avoided as well. Other provisions, words, and phrases to avoid include:

- lengthy instructions and special notes that carve out major exceptions
- complex graduated penalty or suspension rules
- unclear or vague definition of violations

- absence of a defined time frame, such as a statement that the agreement will be amended or renegotiated "soon" after signing
- incentive provisions in which the incentive is an unsafe practice (e.g., "If I obey the Agreement for three straight months, I will be permitted to drive around with my friends on weekend nights.")
- provisions that are contrary to research, such as those that only prohibit passengers "at night" (Numerous studies show that teen passengers of teen drivers increase crash risks at any hour of the day, especially after school lets out.)
- subjects unrelated to driving, such as homework, grades, allowance, life responsibilities, household chores, parental respect, or firearms
- the term *accident* (Among traffic safety professionals and government agencies, the word *crash* is preferred, to emphasize preventability.)
- allowing grace periods for violations, such as a seven-day suspension for arriving home more than forty-five minutes after curfew—which excuses violations of up to forty-four minutes, undermining the standard
- encouraging illegal conduct, such as "If I drink, I will not drive for at least twenty-four hours" (A PTDA should not state that alcohol consumption by those under twenty-one is inevitable, unavoidable, or acceptable.)
- provisions that undermine other sections of the PTDA, such as, "I will obey all state law passenger limits," but later, "I will drive no more than 'x' passengers at any one time."

When drafting a PTDA, each sentence should be considered for enforceability. Drafters should be aware of wording that can cause confusion about a teen driver's conduct and a parent's oversight, including:

- "I will not drive when emotionally upset or when overly tired or angry."
- "I will check in regularly"—which might encourage texting.
- "I will not race, rush, or hurry." An agreement to obey the speed limit and drive appropriately based on road conditions is preferable.
- "I will not drive in bad weather." What is "bad" weather?
- "I will not play around while driving."

A model agreement should be accompanied by a short statement of instructions for its use, including:

- Who signs the agreement? Obviously, the teen driver must sign, but the agreement should also be signed by every adult who will have some role in supervising the teen's driving.
- Where to keep the agreement? Keep one copy of the signed agreement in the car, and one with each person who signed it.
- What about a teen who is already licensed? Can a PTDA be negotiated with a teen who is already licensed and driving? Yes. A violation or crash may provide an opening for a parent to insist on one as a condition of further driving.

There are a number of keys to negotiating a PTDA:

- *Mutual Objectives*: Start with the mind-set that the ultimate, mutual goal is the safety of the driver, passengers, and everyone who shares the road with the teen. A PTDA should be a cooperative process that ends in achievement, not victory.

- *Need to Compromise*: A parent—the person with the keys and thus the power—must make it clear that negotiating and signing an agreement is a nonnegotiable part of the teen being allowed to drive. The parent then needs to show the teen a willingness to be reasonable, to listen, and to accommodate the teen's viewpoint.

- *Single Parents*: When parents are divorced, separated, or otherwise not jointly supervising a teen's driving, it is essential that all who have any supervisory role (such as during visitation) be aware that an agreement exists and what it says, to avoid one parent or supervising adult undermining the PTDA.

- *Vehicle Maintenance*: If a PTDA contains a teen's agreement to "maintain" a vehicle, a few words about what this means will be helpful. At a minimum, safety features such as brakes, wipers, and tires should be identified tasks; a second level is routine upkeep, such as oil changes.

- *Car Keys*: Research shows that teen drivers who have primary or exclusive access to a vehicle have higher crash rates. Car keys are a critical part of a parent's control and leverage. A PTDA should spell out where keys will be kept when the car is not in use.

Turning specifically to the rules that should govern a teen's driving, the following is a list of topics that should be included in every agreement, and why. The specific, recommended wording for each topic can be found in the model agreement at the end of this book.

1. **Time Period**: The agreement should be in effect for a defined minimum period. Teen driver safety research suggests one year from when the teen becomes a licensed driver (that is, authorized to drive solo) as a reasonable period. A more stringent provision is a term of one year or until the teen's eighteenth birthday, whichever is longer. The agreement should state that it will be changed before the stated term ends only if state laws change or the family or teen undergoes a major life change (such as parents separating or divorcing, a geographic move, injury or disability, or a change in economic circumstances).

2. **Parent/Supervising Adult's Overriding Authority**: The agreement should state that parents are ultimately responsible for the safety of their teens, and that supervision of teen driving requires day-by-day judgment, because circumstances can arise in the life of a teen or family such that driving on that particular day will be unsafe. A parent needs to have on-the-spot license suspension authority. This provision also reinforces that teen driving is a privilege, not a right.

3. **Driving Plan**: Supervision of teen drivers is a daily undertaking that has three parts: (1) the teen must ask for permission to drive each and every time; (2) permission should be granted only after parent and teen go through a safety checklist (destination, route, timetable, weather, passengers, and fatigue); and (3) only purposeful driving (driving to a destination for a specific purpose) should be allowed, while joyriding (teens in the car for fun, with no destination or timetable) should be prohibited.

4. **Seat Belts**: Seat belts have been proven repeatedly to be the most effective way for any driver to avoid injury or death. Yet the most recent research shows that approximately 50 percent of teen drivers who die in crashes were not belted. A simple, clear seat belt requirement, no exceptions, is an essential PTDA provision.

The teen driver must wear a seat belt at all times and must require every passenger to wear one as well.

5. **Speeding and Rules of the Road**: Again, it should go without saying that every teen driver will obey traffic laws and signs, as well as the "rules of the road," such as who has the right-of-way (confusion about this is a major cause of teen driver crashes). In addition, the agreement should require drivers to adjust their speed to road conditions such as weather, visibility, and steep slopes.

6. **Cell Phones and Electronic Devices**: The dangers of sending text messages and using handheld cell phones while driving are well documented, as are the reasons the majority of states ban both for teen drivers. However, the latest research also shows that hands-free and voice-activated devices can cause distraction. In addition, many new car models feature dashboard-mounted screens with a variety of interactive features and controls that have raised concerns about distraction. *In a PTDA, the goal should be "zero tolerance" for distraction from cell phones and electronic devices that are unrelated to the safe operation of the vehicle.* The agreement's focus should be to target teen driver *conduct*—that is, the use of these devices *while driving*—rather than trying to list particular (and ever-changing) electronic devices (such as an iPod or laptop). An electronic device provision in a PTDA should be a blanket ban on any use of a device that has the potential to take a teen driver's hands off the wheel, eyes off the road, or mind off the driving situation.

7. **Curfews/Night Driving/Exceptions**: A definitive time, without a grace period, is essential. Most state curfew laws have exceptions, such as school-related activities or employment; each family needs to judge whether teens may need to invoke one of the exceptions (if, for example, the teen has a late-evening job), and the PTDA should account for special circumstances accordingly.

8. **Passengers**: Each and every teen passenger in a teen driver's car adds to the already-high crash risk. Strict limits on teen passengers during at least the first year of licensed driving are a must. While recognizing state law as the baseline, passenger provisions in a PTDA are an opportunity for parents and teens to customize the agreement by establishing a stricter standard. This passenger provision can be further customized to address when a teen driver may transport family members and siblings.

9. **Alcohol or Drug Use, and Fatigue**: Prohibiting a teen from driving while under the influence of alcohol should not require extended discussion, yet about one-third of teen driver fatalities involve alcohol. Every PTDA should say that a teen will "never drive under the influence of alcohol," a phrase intended to recognize that even one drink can impair driving ability. Drugs present a different problem, because there are legal and illegal drugs for teens, and some actually improve driving. For example, teen drivers with attention deficit/hyperactivity disorder face a unique, heightened risk when driving, and we certainly want teens who control their symptoms with prescribed medications to take them. Thus, PTDAs should not ban driving after taking drugs, but rather driving under the influence of illegal or impairing drugs, or an improper dosage of prescribed medication that is unlawful or interferes with reflexes, vision, or reaction time.

Fatigue, also called drowsy driving (see chapter 21), may be the most difficult factor for a parent to monitor (or a teen to recognize or admit), because it can change from day to day or even within the course of one day. Some believe that the answer to fatigue is caffeine or an energy drink, but sleep is the only remedy. Drowsy driving is a major cause of teen driver crashes, and a PTDA requires a clear statement acknowledging this fact as a joint teen-parent responsibility.

10. **Suspension of Driving Privileges**: A critical decision is whether the teen will lose his or her privilege of driving solo, or driving altogether. Will the consequence be to revert to the learner's permit mode? There are two schools of thought here. One is that teens need on-the-road experience, and suspending all driving interferes with continued training. Another is that misconduct should result in no driving at all. Also factored here is how the teen, under a suspension, will get to school, a job, or activities. Some parents will say, "You lost your license, you find a ride." However, the teen then might try to find a ride with a peer in a way that would violate the state's passenger restrictions. This is not an easy issue with a simple answer, but a provision is included in the template PTDA at this end of this book.

11. **Call for a Safe Ride**: To balance the parent override, the agreement should also state that driving privileges will not be suspended if a teen calls for a ride to avoid an unsafe situation.

12. **Costs of Driving**: Driving is expensive, a fact that every teen should learn. Insurance rates for teens have always been much higher than they are for older drivers (and with good reason, given teens' crash rates). Assigning responsibility for driving costs is an important way for parents to control their teen drivers.

13. **Monitoring Technology**: If a parent can afford to install one of the evolving technologies for tracking teen drivers, this should be written into the agreement, with the understanding that data from that device can result in a violation and suspension.

14. **Mediator**: This provision may be most useful for single-parent households, where a trusted intermediary, such as a relative or neighbor, might be needed if parent and teen disagree or reach an impasse about a particular situation.

15. **Other Issues**: In an open-ended "Other Issues" provision, a parent and teen can address which vehicle or vehicles the teen is

permitted to drive, where car keys will be kept, and whether the teen will be permitted to use GPS.

A customizable model parent-teen driving agreement is included at the end of this book.

11

The Difference Between Purposeful Driving and Joyriding

Professional driving instructors offer a key caution that should be obvious but lies just beneath the surface of our consciousness: if a teen has a reason to drive from point A to point B, a prescribed route, an estimated time of arrival, and a consequence for not arriving on time, the likelihood of a serious crash is relatively low. But when teens drive for the sake of driving, without a particular destination, reason, planned route, or arrival time, trouble starts. If teens are driving for fun, to get away from parents or something else at home, to spend time with friends, or perhaps to see just what this four-wheeled contraption can do, crash rates are high.

Simply put, this is the difference between purposeful and recreational driving or what is commonly referred to as joyriding.

If your teen is headed to sports practice or a job and arriving late will result in extra pushups, less playing time, or docked pay, he or she will drive the shortest, quickest route—and will most likely get there safely. If, however, the evening's agenda is a ride "somewhere," to an unknown destination, and with a return time that is merely "sometime before" a curfew, significant motivations for teens to drive safely disappear and factors that can cause a crash take their place. Teens are more likely to practice the safe driving skills they have learned and obey both teen driving and traffic safety laws when their destination is the goal. Conversely, when teens drive for entertainment or escape instead of transportation, safety takes a figurative backseat.

The difference between purposeful and recreational driving will not always be clear. If a teenage boy is driving across town to see his girlfriend and then go to the movies, is that purposeful (the driver has a reason, an estimated arrival time, and a consequence) or recreational? Even so, the vast majority of situations where teens get behind the wheel fall into one category or the other.

Parents are the first line of defense against teen drivers getting into situations where the risk of a crash is heightened. If the driving that your teen proposes today, tonight, or tomorrow can be labeled cruising, joyriding, hanging, hauling, dragging, going for a spin, wheeling, tooling, tracking, scoping, surfing, or some current teen slang equivalent, then think twice about allowing your teen to take the keys and go.

12

Getting a Teen to Acknowledge the Risks

Teenagers often operate in their own private world, focusing on themselves and how they fit in with their peers. Many regard themselves as immune or invulnerable to life's dangers.

Parents are asked to entrust car keys to these limited-vision beings.

So how do we get teen drivers to acknowledge and internalize the risks of driving, and to modify their behavior? Obviously, teens are capable of protecting themselves. They know not to step off a cliff, jump into the path of an oncoming train, or touch a high-voltage wire. How do we get them to recognize driving as another of these clearly understood dangers?

In driver education (whether received from a high school, commercial driving school, or parents/guardians), and in materials provided by motor vehicle departments, schools, police, and advocacy groups, two approaches predominate: gruesome videos and photos, and information about how bad driving decisions will impact teens' families, friends, and communities. Herewith, a strong vote for the second approach.

Not going out on a limb: we would observe that teens in our society are desensitized to blood, guts, gore, body parts, mangled cars, and crash scenes. Millions of people pay money to go to the movies and enjoy the thrill of seeing exactly these things—high-speed car chases, crashes, explosions, and injury and death.

Contrast this approach with teens listening to searing personal testimony from parents, siblings, or friends of teen drivers who have lost their lives or suffered debilitating injuries in car crashes. Every year, parents or "victim advocates" tell high school students about when their teen left the house, how they learned that their teen had been in a serious crash, and how their teen died. They describe the details of the crash and their teen's injuries. They then share their agonizing descent into shock, disbelief, and horror as they realized that there would be no more birthdays, graduations, and weddings.

In our experience, at family victim presentations, when mothers, fathers, and siblings speak, you can hear a pin drop. The students in the audience are not texting or whispering. They are fully engaged in considering their own mortality. They are immersed in the message being delivered and what it would sound like if their own mother, father, sister, or brother were speaking. Tears flow, and invariably students send messages to the presenters about how their remarks have led to changes in their habits as drivers and passengers. Sometimes these teens confess to having near crashes that almost cost them their lives.

The lessons that victim and family advocates provide get teens to internalize the dangers of driving, which is critical. These presentations make the dangers personal and understandable, which according to teens is essential for gaining their trust, buy-in, and subsequent action.

So forget the bloody videos and ask your teen's school to invite an organization or a victim advocate, someone who can deliver a compelling personal story, to speak about the risks of teen driving. Or introduce your teen to someone in your community who is willing to be a real-life example. There are, unfortunately, many people to choose from.

13

The Ceremony of the Keys

I t is standard advice to parents of teen drivers: "You are the keeper of the keys." Let's explore what this means.

In general, of course, no keys means no car. If parents withhold keys, teens don't drive, and there are no teen driver crashes. But except for putting off driving to a more mature age, parents may wonder when, where, and how to hand over the car keys to their teens.

The starting point is to keep in mind the powerful if not exalted position of being a parent. A parent is the dragon that guards the treasure. No one gets by who shouldn't. Parents are the parole board that decides who gets released and when. They decide whether an inexperienced and risk-prone person will be allowed to operate a piece of heavy machinery that has the potential to injure or kill others. Parents hold a position of responsibility to our families and to everyone else who will be on the same street or highway as our teen drivers.

What should a teen need to do to obtain the keys? First and foremost, he must *have to ask for them*. Keys should not be readily available to any teen driver. They should not be just one more article in the bin on the kitchen counter. To go back to the air traffic controller analogy (see chapter 9), the exercise of a teen asking for the keys each time he wants to get behind the wheel is a parent's opportunity to review the flight plan and conduct a safety check. Weather suitable for an inexperienced driver? Destination and time of arrival and departure established? Route mapped out? Driver rested, alert, and not overly stressed? The teen's trip should be purposeful, not recreational (see chapter 11). The main points of the parent-teen driving agreement (see chapter 10) should be briefly reviewed. *Handing over the keys should be a ceremony that highlights the seriousness of the activity at hand.*

If that sounds a bit extreme (some might call it helicopter parenting), think back to your teen driving years. We're betting that before you ran out the door, at least one parent asked you three simple but important questions: Where are you going? Who are you going with? When will you be home? While you may have been annoyed by this inquisition, the interruption was extremely important. Research has confirmed that teens who must ask for the keys are less likely to crash.

Where should a parent keep the keys? Hiding them is one option (although Tim concedes that on occasion, he forgot where he hid the keys). Concealing the keys may only set off a game of hide-and-seek. The hiding might also underscore a lack of trust and undermine the also-important message that driving is a very adult action.

On the other hand, it is hard to advocate that the keys be available in your teen's plain sight, governed only by an understanding—even if stated in the parent-teen driving agreement—that he will ask for the keys each time before driving. There should be a middle ground. We advocate having the keys available on a stand-alone hook, in plain sight of supervising parents, so everyone knows when the keys are there and when they have been taken. Perhaps the "Tips from Tim and Pam" list at the end of this book (see chapter 28) will be taped to the wall next to the key hook. In this way, their location is not secret, but taking them will be a deliberate, contemplative, public step. This system, we think, emphasizes that the keys are being made available in return for a renewed safety review and pledge.

Whether handing over the keys is tied to other matters such as completion of homework and chores is your business, but our view is that driving is driving and, like parent-teen driving agreements, should be separate from other parent-teen matters. We have enough to think about when it comes to teen driving without mixing in other parts of life.

Being the custodian of the keys is a somewhat different undertaking when your teen is the primary driver of the car, as opposed to one of several drivers of a family car. Research has demonstrated that teens who have their own vehicles have higher crash rates than those who rely on a parent's or sibling's car (see chapter 18). This advice about keys, therefore, is doubly important if your teen has his own car.

Car keys are a parent's leverage. Use it. Make each time your teen gets behind the wheel an investiture ceremony, a conferring of knighthood. Keep firmly in mind what is at stake and what is at risk.

14

The Unappreciated Danger of Passengers, Even Siblings

Oone of the saddest realities of teen driver crashes is that other teens who may be riding in the vehicle are often killed. Crashes like Reid's, where the teen driver was killed but the passengers survived, are the exception.

The simple, well-documented fact is that teen crash risk—which is already high, due to inexperience and incomplete brain development—increases when just one teen passenger is in the vehicle, and escalates with each additional passenger.

Passengers distract a teen driver. This distraction occurs when the driver engages in conversation, debates music choices, or talks about what's happening inside and outside the vehicle. In some cases, passengers may even physically interfere with the driver (e.g., show the driver something on a phone), or their presence may prompt speeding, tailgating, or showing off.

This is why a passenger restriction is a key provision of graduated driver licensing. But note that passenger restrictions vary by state, with some having no rules at all and others allowing passengers just three months after a teen is licensed. As a result, parents need to learn their state's law regarding passengers, and then often intervene with stricter rules.

Distraction caused by passengers is particularly problematic for teenage boys and is one reason that teen males are twice as likely as teen females to be involved in a fatal crash. (This isn't surprising since all males, not just teens, are more likely to engage in unsafe driving and to crash and die as a result. While data suggest that females are starting to catch up—women overall are driving 89 percent farther than they did four decades ago—men still do a majority of the driving on American roads.) A recent analysis of teen-involved fatal crashes by the Governors Highway Safety Association found that the gap between male and female teen drivers has remained relatively constant over the past ten years, with males accounting for an average of 70 percent of the crashes and females the remaining 30 percent. Thus, being the passenger of a teenage male driver is a higher risk compared to a female teen driver.

The clear evidence about teen drivers and passengers highlights the fact that parents are in the best position to supervise a teen driver's passengers. Enforcement of passenger restrictions by parents offers the greatest potential for reduction of current crash levels. And, as noted, the more lenient a state's passenger rules, the more vigilant a parent must be.

The fact that driving is the leading cause of death of people under twenty in the United States also prompts this question: At what age do kids begin to be at risk as passengers? National statistics provide the answer: age twelve. Junior high school. Another question: During what time of day are teen passengers most at risk? Here too the answer is clear: the hours directly after school, when kids are most likely to pile into cars without parents present to say, "Not so fast," and with freedom and fun most on their minds.

Parents who conclude that it is safe for their child to ride with a teen driver because that driver is a "sensible kid" who has taken driver's ed are playing with fire. The best advice about riding with a teen driver is *don't*.

But since this may happen, the fallback is to identify the factors that increase the baseline dangers of teen driving: recreational driving (driving without a destination, a prescribed route, a timetable, and a consequence for arriving late), distracted driving (texting, using an electronic device, or doing anything that takes eyes off the road, hands off the wheel, or mind off the situation), impaired driving (drugs, alcohol), drowsy driving, driving at night or in bad weather, driving in an unfamiliar place, and driving without a seat belt. At least avoid these higher-risk situations.

An adult driver who is specifically supervising a teen driver and is sitting in the front passenger seat can be regarded as a second pair of eyes. However, to think that a teen passenger or anyone in the backseat improves safety by being an additional pair of eyes is simply inaccurate. The potential for distraction outweighs the additional vigilance.

Some parents justify allowing teen drivers to have illegal passengers because it saves on gas. We wonder how many times a teen passenger actually pays for a share of gas, but in any event, the cost of gasoline is trivial compared to the documented dangers—and the personal and financial cost—of teen drivers having passengers. The same is true of the explanation that a teen driver needs passengers to get experience driving with passengers. Teens should learn to become safe drivers first; then they can move on to learning to drive safely with passengers.

Passengers are a topic for which it is simple for parents to set down clear rules: No passengers that are illegal under state law. No passengers without the express permission of the parent/ supervising adult of the teen driver and the passenger. No exceptions, and this should be clear in a parent-teen driving agreement.

If your child must ride with a teen, don't allow him or her to get in a car with a teen driver who is not known to you—as best you can determine—as an experienced driver (at least one year with a full license and no suspensions or crashes) who legally may carry passengers. Only purposeful driving should be allowed; joy-rides should be prohibited. *Communicate with the driver's parent or supervising adult so everyone is aware of the plan.* Explain to your teen not to tolerate any form of distraction or impairment by the teen driver. Rehearse a strategy for how your teen, as a passenger, will get out of the car if the situation becomes unsafe (the most popular is "I feel like I am going to throw up"). Have a code word that your teen can text or say in a phone call if he or she is in danger. Make it clear that the decision to get out of the car of a distracted, impaired, drowsy, or unsafe driver, even in the middle of nowhere, can be the difference between life and death. And don't forget that pets can be dangerous distractions too.

The last passenger issue is siblings. Although the passenger restrictions of many GDL laws allow teens to transport their siblings earlier than other passengers, research shows that the distraction risk is equally great. Minimum age rules for licenses, unfortunately, are based more on tradition than science or traffic safety facts. *Allowing siblings as passengers of newly licensed teen drivers is guaranteed to increase crash rates and put both teen drivers and their siblings at risk.* If laws were based on current research and statistics, siblings would not be allowed as passengers earlier than others.

Siblings as passengers are as distracting as nonsiblings, and in some cases more so. Ask yourself this question: Do your children butt heads and get under each other's skin? Probably. Now imagine them in a car, with one of them behind the wheel. Can the driver really stay focused on the road?

Driving instructors have explained to us that new drivers are still in learning mode and should not be distracted by siblings while they are learning. Learning to drive with the distractions of passengers is a skill for later in a driver's development. The safety concern is indisputable and should trump all other factors. As a noted traffic researcher once observed, "Would you trust your most precious cargo to your most inexperienced driver?"

15

Managing Curfews

Teen driver laws in most states set nighttime restrictions or curfews that dictate when teen drivers can and can't be on the road. In general, the deadline for teen drivers to be off the road ranges from 9:00 PM to midnight. (The most common is 11:00 PM or midnight to 5:00 or 6:00 AM.) Most state laws, however, contain exceptions for employment, school activities, medical needs, religious observances, and participation in volunteer public safety services (fire, ambulance, "safe rides," and the like), each of which can necessitate driving in the late evening or early morning.

While your state GDL law may include one or more of these exemptions, the exceptions are not based on evidence or less risk. According to the Centers for Disease Control and Prevention, one third of fatal teen crashes occur after dark, with 51 percent happening before midnight. Parents need to determine if a teen is really ready for night driving, and not feel compelled to allow it in a particular situation simply because state law authorizes it.

Here are some thoughts on driving curfews and how to manage them:

- Curfews do not address the dangerous one or two hours after school. It is at those times that teens are most likely to be riding with illegal passengers, which substantially increases crash risk. Curfews only target late-night driving, but the hours immediately after school are also a time of elevated crash risk.
- As to late-night driving, a constant problem is teen drivers racing home to beat the curfew. In fact, some teens think that getting off the road by the state's deadline is a legitimate reason to drive at whatever speed is necessary to get home on time.
- Curfews do not justify speeding, of course, but they do highlight the importance of planning ahead so that teens will be off the road without speeding. Doing so requires a discussion, before the teen leaves, about the route and the anticipated return trip travel time. Once these are established, parent and teen are better able to plan to comply with the curfew. The departure should also build in a margin for traffic delay; if the route normally takes thirty minutes and the curfew is 11:00 PM, then departure time should be 10:15 PM.
- The teen driver should understand that a delay such as a traffic backup that will result in missing the curfew needs to be reported to a parent or guardian as soon as it can be done safely. That means not texting or using a cell phone while driving, but pulling off the road to a safe location at the earliest opportunity to explain the location and extent of the delay. The teen should understand that delays

first reported upon arrival at home will be thoroughly questioned.

- School events and activities that end after 9:00 PM are a significant problem, because they result in teens driving during the most dangerous hours of the day, often with passengers and when fatigue is likely. Supervising adults should realize that they may need to be chauffeurs even to newly licensed drivers to avoid this dangerous situation. Pam regularly did this for her son, a high school ice hockey player, who sometimes had games that ended well after 9:00 PM (some 11:00 PM or later).

- If the parent and teen have executed a parent-teen driving agreement, they have most likely identified a penalty for missing a curfew. This provision requires a parent's judgment. As we all know, predicting driving time is an inexact science, and there will be times when teens will arrive late due to conditions beyond their control. Recall that the purpose of a PTDA is a mutual commitment to safety, not a punishment for the slightest infraction. If the teen was diligent in leaving on time, provides a credible explanation for being a few minutes late, and is not a repeat offender, flexibility is appropriate.

- As for managing the exceptions to curfews stated in your state's law, the first simple rule is: if the teen will be on the road after the state's curfew on a regular basis, most likely for employment or a school activity, have the employer or a school official provide a letter, on letterhead, that the teen can keep in the glove box. The letter should specify when the teen will be on the road, why, and the route. An employer's letter might say: "To Whom It May Concern/Law Enforcement: Kevin Jones is an employee of the 7-Eleven Store on Midland Avenue in Smithtown. He works until midnight on Friday, Saturday, and Sunday, after which he drives to his home at 123 Main Street, using Route 14." A school official's letter might say: "Mary Doe is involved in a theater production at Central High School from April 16 to May 4. She will leave school Monday through Thursday night between 11:00 PM and midnight and drive to her home at 18 Elm Street, using the River Parkway." However, this letter should never be treated as permission to drive to a destination other than home.

- Teens need to understand the limits on using exceptions. When Tim speaks to high school students, he tells them: "If the curfew is 11:00 PM and it's 11:15 PM because the game went into overtime, and the police stop you, but you are somewhere close to a direct line between school and your home, you're not breaking the law. But if it's 2:00 AM and you're two towns away, you're in trouble."

- Parents should bear in mind that a joyride with a curfew is still a joyride and therefore dangerous. The fact that a teen may be ordered home from joyriding (see chapter 11) by a certain time does not lessen the huge dangers of the joyride itself.

- Finally, recognize that the nighttime curfew in a state's teen driver law is a *minimum*. Use your judgment on a case-by-case basis. Exercise your rights under your parent-teen driving agreement. Err on the side of earlier than state law (such as 9:00 PM for new drivers) and allow exceptions only when justified. If particular circumstances such as fatigue or bad weather compel you to set an earlier curfew on a particular evening, by all means do so.

As with all other parts of teen driver laws, the state sets one curfew for all teens in all circumstances. This does not mean that you, as a parent, park your judgment in the garage.

16

Supervising the Brand-New Driver

Although parents would like to believe that training teen drivers is a linear equation, that teens become better drivers as they log more hours behind the wheel, it is well documented that *driving deteriorates when teens begin to drive unsupervised*—not because skills deteriorate but because attitudes change. During the first six months that teens drive solo, with no one there to monitor or correct them, they are prone to experiment and jettison whatever parts of instruction they think are stupid. In particular, brand-new drivers take aim at parent hypocrisy, adopting the bad driving habits that parents or guardians warned them about because the parents regularly made these mistakes as well. In fact, this phenomenon most highlights the facts that parents are role models for young drivers, and at no time is a parent's own driving more consequential than when a teen has a learner's permit. Parents can count on the fact that their teen is watching. If parents use distracting electronics, don't buckle up, speed, tailgate, don't signal, or drive impaired, they should *expect* their teens to copy them when they begin driving by themselves. Our recommendation: always be the driver you want your teen to be.

So, just when parents may think that their teens are doing fine—no crash yet—they should be more vigilant than ever, because some teens' training evaporates when they drive unsupervised.

There is no magic solution to this dilemma, but three approaches may help. The first is to provide your teen far more on-the-road training hours than state law requires. Perhaps if a teen has hundreds of hours at the wheel instead of the twenty to fifty that most states require, he or she will have more ingrained good habits and overall skill. The next is for parents to realize that a teen beginning to drive unsupervised is not the end of supervised training. The first two years of driving are the most dangerous for teens, with the risk highest during the first thirty to ninety days of independent driving. For this reason, parents should slowly ease their teens into this stage, alternating supervised and unsupervised driving for the first several months.

A third way, if affordable, is to install one of the teen driver tracking technologies. Those that report on the car's speed and location and can even set geographic boundaries for the teen driver's vehicle are the most important at the start. Teens whose unsupervised driving is electronically monitored will be, by definition and in result, more accountable.

Obviously, these systems continue to evolve and improve, such that any detailed description of capabilities could be outdated in a matter of months. Suffice it to say that, basically, these systems electronically track vehicle location and speed and transmit a report to supervising adults. Some systems use boxes that rest on the dashboard (which can give sneaky teens a way to evade them), while others are hardwired into the vehicle. Some track and report in "real time" (every few minutes) while others generate periodic (such as monthly) reports. A few systems, not unlike electric fences for pets, set geographic boundaries and give the teen a warning signal and supervising adults a report if the vehicle breaches the set boundaries.

If parents can afford them, these systems are a useful tool for managing teen drivers. A teen's knowledge that his or her driving conduct is being electronically monitored can only help. Moreover, any teen who tries to disable or outsmart a tracking system will surely raise a red flag about not being ready to take safe driving seriously.

So, with the caveat that these systems are in no way a basis for parents to otherwise let their guard down, tracking technology, if affordable, is a sensible proactive step.

Traffic Tickets as Teachable Moments

Picture this: Your teen, a licensed driver for several months, receives a ticket from a police officer for violating some provision of your state's teen driver laws—speeding, carrying too many passengers, driving after curfew, violating cell phone restrictions, committing a moving violation. The teen pleads with you that she didn't do it or the police made a mistake or the officer singled her out from among other drivers whose driving was much worse because she's a teenager. Or the police were sneaky, lying in wait to catch someone. "It's just not fair!" pleads your young driver. This was her first direct encounter with the police.

A teen driver receiving a ticket sets three things in motion. First, parent and teen need to talk through what happened (and get past the initial denials). Second, the teen driver and parent need to decide whether they will challenge the ticket or accept the consequences—paying a fine, incurring driving record points, or receiving a license suspension. Third, parent and teen need to decide *when* they are going to respond.

This third decision is important—there is almost always an administrative lag time between when police issue a ticket and when the government processes the driver's response or a court issues a hearing date.

Every state administers tickets differently for driving violations. Weeks or even months can elapse between when a ticket is issued to a teen driver and when she receives notice of the penalty for a violation or notice of a court date. Meanwhile, unless the parent and teen have signed a teen driving agreement that results in an immediate suspension, or the parent imposes an on-the-spot suspension, the teen may continue to drive.

For the parent of a teen driver, this situation is a critical teachable moment. At stake are your teen's respect for the law in general, teen driver laws in particular, and law enforcement; and her understanding that driving is a public rather than a personal act that impacts the safety of other people on the road. How you address each of these issues will affect your teen's approach to driving.

This concern about parent conduct and guidance is not hypothetical. In 2007, Massachusetts adopted a mandatory license suspension system for teens who violated its GDL laws. Suspensions started at sixty days for a first offense and went up from there for repeat offenses. Within months of the start of enforcement, the news media began to report about parents resisting fiercely—screaming at prosecutors and court personnel, doing everything possible to avoid suspensions of their teens' licenses. These parents were no doubt angry about the inconvenience of once again having to drive their teens to school and events, and losing their new in-house pickup and delivery service. But what struck us about these news articles was envisioning the teens standing there, watching their parents challenge and disparage police, prosecutors, court staff, and even judges.

We recognize that police can make mistakes and that sometimes they use enforcement techniques such as speed traps that can seem unfair. Police can appear arbitrary when ticketing some while letting other offenders go unpunished. Moreover, a police officer stopping a teen driver can create the perception that the teen has been profiled; that is, stopped due to his or her apparent age rather than driving conduct.

But back to the teachable moment and the three issues: While parents should review with their teens the events that led to the ticket, they should also recognize that factually baseless tickets are a relatively rare occurrence. One of the best assurances we have that tickets issued to teen drivers usually have some actual basis is that the police generally have far more responsibilities than they can handle; they issue tickets when misconduct genuinely threatens public safety.

If we assume that most tickets have some basis, then we can focus on the key point: a parent's reaction to a teen driver's ticket presents a critical opportunity to reinforce several safe driving lessons. So, parents, please don't disparage the teen driving laws or law enforcement; argue with law enforcement, prosecutors, or court staff about your teen's conduct; let inconvenience or cost to you get in the way of these lessons; or delay having your teen take the medicine. Don't ask a court for repeated continuances (delays), and don't make excuses ("she has a quiz/game/lesson") that pale in comparison to safety.

Another, somewhat hidden side of the situation after law enforcement issues a ticket is the time it can take from when the ticket is issued to when it is enforced through a fine or license suspension by a motor vehicle department or the court system. Most states and some big cities have a central processing bureau, so that when the police issue a ticket, the ticket is sent to that bureau, which sends a notice of the violation to the teen driver's home. Whether parents should be notified when their teen drivers receive tickets, are involved in a crash, or have their licenses suspended or revoked is an interesting policy or administrative issue. A few states have parent notification programs. Some states issue a warning letter to a teen upon receipt of a first ticket. Putting parents and new teen drivers on notice about the dangers of engaging in unlawful, unsafe behaviors behind the wheel is important, because a young driver's chance of being involved in a crash doubles after a first violation.

If the punishment is only a monetary fine, the teen either pays the fine and that is the end of it, or goes to court to contest the fine, which may result in a reduction or a deal with a prosecutor. In some states, paying the fine is an admission of wrongdoing that results in an automatic license suspension. If the penalty is license suspension, the driver either accepts the suspension, sends in the acknowledgment, has the license suspended, and then endures the no-license period, or the driver goes to court, seeking to have the suspension modified or reversed. Finally, in some states, a ticket or a repeat violation triggers mandatory driver retraining: the teen driver reports to the motor vehicle department or a driving school for a refresher. But the question is: What should a parent do with a teen driver while the police, the motor vehicle department, the processing agency, and the court system sort all of this out? First, this situation illustrates one key benefit of a parent-teen driving agreement. If a parent and teen have negotiated and signed one, it provides the first answer, an immediate suspension of driving for some period of time as stated in the agreement, regardless of whether or when the government acts. (In the model agreement in this book, this immediate suspension is in addition to whatever the government imposes, so that misconduct has two penalties.)

Second is to realize that the issuance of a ticket should be a loud alarm that a teen is at risk, especially if the violation involved something like speeding, carrying illegal passengers, not wearing a seat belt, consuming alcohol or drugs, or similar serious offenses. In other words, don't let the fact that the government takes time to impose a punishment lull you as a parent into taking the violation as anything less than a serious development requiring your own immediate discipline and increased oversight.

The administrative delay that can follow a teen getting a ticket should not cause parents to let their guard down. If anything, it should go way, way up.

18

Car Buying and Sharing, and Saving on Gas

While the title of this chapter could suggest that choosing a particular make and model car somehow overcomes the risks discussed in previous chapters, this is not the case. The best advice we can offer on this topic is *the best car for a teen may well be no car.* We concede, however, that life demands may require bowing to but then proactively managing reality, so we offer the following accumulated wisdom on this topic.

The best practice here is simple. Cars with the most safety features are the best. Consider these characteristics for a teen driver's car:

- air bags (driver, front passenger, side, curtain)
- crash ratings
- electronic stability control and antilock brakes (standard on 2012 and newer models)

- horsepower (over 300 is considered "high performance"—and dangerous for an inexperienced driver)
- vehicle weight to horsepower ratio (which some experts say should be less than 15:1)
- rollover ratings (SUVs and pickup trucks have higher centers of gravity, making them more susceptible to rollovers)
- acceleration (zero to sixty in at least eight but no more than eleven seconds)
- braking distance
- visibility on all sides from the driver's seat (which means no or few blind spots)
- back-up camera
- steel reinforced doors
- impact-absorbing designs and materials

Automobile technology is evolving, and manufacturers are introducing new safety features every year. Experts continually evaluate these new devices to see if they improve safety and are cost-effective. In the meantime, if you are considering buying a new or used car for a teen, or allowing a teen to buy one, the best advice is to consider whether the purchase can be postponed, and the second best is to be sure the vehicle includes as many of the safety features listed above as possible. For help understanding the latest vehicle technologies and their benefits, visit the websites of the AAA Foundation for Traffic Safety, the National Safety Council, and the Insurance Institute for Highway Safety.

Parents and teens also should not neglect old-fashioned basics; the car should be outfitted with supplies for emergencies and bad weather: extra motor oil and windshield fluid, battery cables, a small fire extinguisher, a tire pressure gauge, a flashlight, a pen and pad, an ice scraper/brush, a snow shovel, kitty litter or sand (for traction when stuck on ice or snow), water, nonperishable snacks, a blanket, gloves, and duct tape. Store these items in a duffle bag or old suitcase in the trunk or behind the last row of seats to keep them organized, accessible, and out of harm's way. Remember that all loose items in a vehicle become flying debris in the event of a crash.

As to buying a car for a teen driver, research establishes this further caution for parents: *teens who are permitted to have their own cars or to be the primary drivers of a particular car have higher crash rates than those who share a car with a parent or another family member.* A leading research hospital offers these frightening statistics:

- Almost three out of every four teen drivers in the United States have "primary access" to a vehicle (meaning they can drive the car whenever they want, so long as they can obtain the keys and permission; that is, they do not have to wait for someone else to finish using the vehicle).
- Teens with primary access to a car drive about 6.6 hours and 200 miles per week, compared to 130 miles in 4.3 hours for those who share a car.
- Crash rates for teens with primary access to a car are more than double compared to their counterparts who rely on a shared or family car.

This research presents a statistical case against giving teens primary access, but it seems to us that the reasons for this marked difference go beyond what can be demonstrated statistically. If a teen shares a car with a parent, the following good things are likely to happen: the parent keeps a closer watch on whether and when the teen gets behind the wheel; the parent is more likely to be attuned to the difference between purposeful and recreational driving; the teen is more likely to have to ask for the keys from the parent; the parent is more likely to make an informed, day-by-day, case-by-case judgment on whether it is safe for the teen to drive; the parent and teen are more likely, before the teen leaves, to put together at least an informal plan for the driving route, passengers, arrival time, check-in time, and return time; and the parent and teen are more likely to consider, at least momentarily, whether driving at that particular moment is allowed under their parent-teen driving agreement.

At a basic parent-teen level, it seems that when a teen shares a car with a parent, that parent is more motivated to be proactive than a parent whose teen has his or her own car. This occurs if only to protect the value of the car and the parent's own convenience. Conversely, teens just don't want to face the consequences of crashing a parent's car.

The research to date, then, is simple, clear, and in line with common sense: buying your teen his or her own car, or giving your teen primary access to a car, substantially increases the risk of a crash, injury, or fatality. By contrast, forcing a teen to share a car reinforces good parenting and oversight across the board.

And then there is the price of gasoline. In the past several years, of course, costs have risen dramatically, only to then fall just as quickly. Either way, the price of gas is a push and pull, a double-edged sword, for teen driver safety.

Teen driver crash rates have been declining modestly but steadily during the past several years. Undoubtedly, stricter GDL laws and more attentive parents are contributing factors, but more expensive gasoline and the economic recession also have been influences. Obviously, as driving becomes more expensive, all drivers, and especially teens and people whose income has declined, drive fewer miles. By definition, this translates into fewer crashes and fatalities. Moreover, in difficult economic times, when jobs for teens are more scarce, teens are separated from a key source of gas money. Fewer jobs for teens and less income mean less driving and fewer crashes and injuries.

The high cost of refueling also has the benefit of limiting teens to purposeful driving and reducing joyriding. Parents clamp down out of economic necessity, not just safety, on their teens taking the car to hang out with friends. In this way, more expensive gas directly reduces a mode of teen driving—without a purpose, route, timetable, and consequence for arriving late—that is among the most dangerous for teens.

On the other hand, there are safety downsides to more expensive gas. The first is that teens get less practice behind the wheel; instruction itself has become more financially burdensome. Another negative is that parents are economically motivated to bend or violate state driving laws. Passenger restrictions have a cost: expensive gas gives parents a reason to combine driving practice with times when siblings and other illegal passengers are in the car, even if this practice is against the law. Paradoxically then, gas prices get in the way of the precious hours of practice that teen driver laws promote, and this can lead parents to set a bad example by allowing teens to drive in illegal situations.

A third significant result of the cost of gas for teen drivers is the incentive to share the pump price with passengers. As research clearly shows, teen driver crash rates go up substantially with each additional passenger who is not an instructor or supervisor. On the other hand, four dollars per gallon and higher gas prices, especially for teens driving every day to school, a job, or other daily activities, is a compelling reason to divide the expense with passengers, even if they are illegal and unsafe.

High gas prices require every family to make hard choices about important matters—as basic as where we live in relation to jobs, schools, services, and stores. Yet as difficult as these decisions can be, for parents of teen drivers who put safety ahead of cost, the choices are clear:

- Use gas prices to help your teens learn the reality that driving can be expensive.
- Take the reduction in teen driving that results from high gas prices as a net gain for safety.
- Don't give in to the temptation to use high gas prices as an excuse to violate teen driver laws.
- Accept that high gas prices give parents another good reason to say no to teens who want to go for a joyride.
- Understand that when calculating the costs of gas against the costs of injury or even loss of life, there is simply no comparison.

19

Distracted Driving: Texting, "Connected Cars," GPS, and Headphones

D istracted driving resulting from the use of electronic devices is a national epidemic. The federal government, traffic safety advocates, schools, insurance companies, and even personal injury lawyers have identified it as a significant danger that puts all roadway users at risk. The public agrees that distracted driving is dangerous, but that has not been translated into action, with nearly three-quarters of teens and adults adopting a "Do as I say, not as I do" attitude. In fact, the most recent federal government data indicate that teens account for the largest proportion of drivers who were distracted at the time of a fatal crash.

Parents of teen drivers need to know three things about distracted driving: what it is, why it is so dangerous, and what rules they should enforce with their teens.

A common definition of distracted driving is hands off the wheel, eyes off the road, or mind off the driving situation. The first two are easy to understand: reaching into the backseat or trying to read a map while driving are common distractions. The third is more subtle. Scientists have documented that when drivers—of any age—are engaged in a conversation, up to one-third of their brain function is diverted from evaluating the traffic situation ahead. In other words, talking to a passenger while driving detracts attention to the road. Conversations about emotional or heated topics are, of course, the most distracting. The technical term for driving with eyes open and hands on the wheel but with diminished attention to road conditions is *cognitive blindness*.

The primary danger of distracted driving is that it negatively affects the driver's reaction time necessary to avoid a crash. At 30 mph, a car travels 143 feet in three seconds. At 60 mph, it's 286 feet, almost the length of a football field. Avoiding a crash requires three steps: (1) comprehending the danger, (2) executing a maneuver to evade the danger, and (3) either slowing down or stopping the vehicle. In many instances, for an alert, responsive driver, each of the first two steps can take about one second. The third depends on speed, vehicle weight, and road conditions, but usually requires several seconds. Thus, if a driver traveling at 60 mph is distracted for even three seconds, the car covers the length of a football field with no opportunity for the driver to take even the first step in avoiding a crash.

It is impossible to emphasize sufficiently how important it is for parents to warn and train their teens about the dangers of distracted driving. *Distraction and inattention, as much as speed, alcohol, or passengers, are primary causes of teen driver crashes.* According to a recent study, many teens do not comprehend the danger; nearly 30 percent surveyed did not regard taking their eyes off the road for up to ten seconds as an unsafe behavior. Teen drivers need their visual, manual, and cognitive abilities and every bit of time available to help them discern the traffic situation and respond appropriately. *Thus, prohibiting the use of any electronic device not crucial to the safe operation of the vehicle must be the rule for teens—no exceptions.* Put another way, no texting, typing, reading, watching a video, making a phone call, or taking a selfie when the car is not in park.

Three caveats go along with this ironclad electronic device rule. The first is that there are ways for parents to check whether their teens are using an electronic device, especially a cell phone, while driving. One of the realities of technology today is that it leaves a cyber footprint. Supervising adults should not hesitate to go online with their service provider and perform a postdriving review of the phone itself, or at least review monthly statements to check on a teen driver's cell phone use, paying particular attention to time of day (which can be obtained from the service provider).

Second, parents should understand that state motor vehicle laws about use of electronic devices (for both teens and adult drivers) are a patchwork nationally and often difficult to follow. For example, many state laws ban the use of cell phones but allow the use of "audio equipment" while driving. So may a teen driver use an iPod—audio equipment—while driving? The point is that, in this area in particular, *parents should ignore state law's definitions and exemptions and simply impose a "no device/no use" rule.*

A third caution is that teen drivers should use an electronic device only when they have stopped the car, meaning the car is in park. Despite what a teen may think, a car in gear but stopped by a foot on the brake is still a vehicle capable of moving and thus a risk that requires the driver's full attention.

It is essentially pointless to talk here about particular devices, such as apps that disable cell phones and texting while a vehicle is in motion. (We advise parents to be leery of apps that claim to offer the solution to distracted driving.) To write about today's technologies is to be outdated just months from now; indeed, one of the follies of state legislatures passing laws that purport to restrict or ban particular gadgets in cars is that these laws quickly become outdated. It's silly to parse the ever-changing particulars of in-vehicle devices; all we can do is heighten parents' consciousness of the added risks of the various and evolving electronics.

Apps that disable cell phones or texting while driving are helpful in that they delay risky conduct, but we should not trust a technology whose purpose is to undo other technology. Installing technology and apps that disable the use of cell phones and texting when a car is in motion is the equivalent of placing a bomb inside the car—but then giving the driver a tool to defuse it. These apps make the double assumption that teens will drive *and* text, and the solution is to give them an additional piece of technology to counteract the danger that the first technology creates. *Parents should consider whether a teen who is likely to text while driving should ever get behind the wheel.*

Unrealistic? Maybe, but our point is that in-vehicle technologies that try to counteract potentially deadly behavior are missing a critical point: our first priority must be to separate our new drivers from the inherent dangers. Accepting them and then trying to mitigate them is the next level, but should not be the starting point.

In any event, "texting" is any act of typing or reading on a screen while driving. It doesn't matter what device is used, whether the keystrokes are on a handheld phone, a dashboard-mounted screen, or a laptop computer. It doesn't matter whether the typing is in an Internet search bar or a message window. Dialing a phone while driving is a form of texting. Reading anything on a screen is also considered texting.

Texting is the most dangerous form of distracted driving because it involves all three of the highest-risk behaviors: the texter takes his eyes off the road, at least one hand off the wheel, and his mind off the driving situation.

Traffic safety researchers at Virginia Tech have calculated that a driver (again, of any age) who texts—types or reads—while driving is twenty-three times more likely to crash. The primary reason is that *the average act of sending a text message takes about five seconds, and thus completely eliminates the three-second minimum reaction time needed to avoid a crash.*

Volumes have been written about texting. State and federal lawmakers have struggled to define it, but it's really very simple: no one should ever type or read on a screen while driving. Period.

While distracted driving is often characterized as a teen and young driver phenomenon arising from texting, new distracting technologies are moving into the adult driver mainstream. Auto manufacturers are adding distracting electronics, mainly as dashboard-mounted, multipurpose, interactive computer screens that offer not only telecommunications, navigation, and sound systems but also consumer electronics, video entertainment, and interactive Internet connections that allow use of social media. *Consumer Reports* has dubbed vehicles equipped with interactive technology "connected cars." One auto manufacturer has described its goal as "iPhones with wheels." The functions, sophistication, and availability of these systems are limited only by the imaginations and collaborations of electronics and auto industry engineers and consumer preferences and budgets, but there does not appear to be any doubt that dashboards will be the location, big screens will be the basic installation, distracting interactive functions will be the norm, and entirely preventable crashes and fatalities will be the result.

Predicting the exact shape of these imminent amenities is not our focus. The point is that while research is pouring in about the dangers of distracted driving, electronics and auto manufacturing companies are working as quickly as they can to introduce new features into cars that, we can predict with certainty, will compromise safety.

It appears that the universal defense from manufacturers is that they are only responding to consumer demand, and safety "is a matter of individual responsibility." In other words, if your car comes with a dashboard-mounted screen that allows you, while driving on an interstate, to launch a browser, search for the nearest restaurant, and display reviews of its food and service, then it is simply up to you as a driver to do so responsibly and safely.

The fallacy of this argument, of course, is that driving, more than any other activity in our society, implicates the safety of others. In no other activity does one person randomly threaten more people than when a driver takes his eyes off the road to interact with a screen.

Thus, we have ongoing today, simultaneously, nationwide efforts to not only improve safety but also introduce into cars new technologies that will cause death and serious injury in exactly the ways that so many are trying to prevent. Distractions from electronic devices are not just a young driver problem but also an adult driver phenomenon. Parents of teen drivers should keep in mind the implications of this trend: *parents are role models, and those who surf the Internet with their eyes and fingers while driving will have a harder time warning their teens about the dangers of texting.*

Which leads us to the most problematic device for teen drivers: the global positioning system, or GPS. Both of us have been asked by driver training professionals, parents, and even teens about whether state laws banning teen drivers from using any "mobile electronic device" includes GPS. This seemingly straightforward question turned out to be rather complex. On the one hand, a GPS helps us with directions, and so it is a safety aid. On the other hand, a GPS is an electronic device with a screen and thus exactly the kind of distraction from driving that causes crashes. Can these contradictory uses both be correct?

Many state teen driver laws prohibit the use of any "mobile or wireless electronic device" while driving. These laws also often refer to "any handheld or hands-free or other portable electronic equipment," thereby including any texting device, pager, personal digital assistant, laptop computer, or video game. However, these definitions sometimes exclude equipment "installed for the purpose of providing navigation."

A GPS "provides navigation," right? But use of distracting electronic devices is strictly prohibited. So, if a teen driver takes his or her eyes off the road to type in an address on a GPS, is he or she violating the law?

It appears that some state laws do not consider a GPS to be the type of electronic device that teen drivers should be prohibited from using, while others do. But let us as parents and instructors of teen drivers consider whether using a GPS is a good idea, legal or not.

GPS units are amazing devices that provide directions to our destination and pinpoint the location of our vehicle. The safety advantage can be substantial to drivers, emergency responders, and law enforcement. Yet consider these drawbacks:

- Unless the GPS is voice-activated, using one requires typing in an address, which is no different from, and every bit as dangerous as, texting if it occurs while the car is in motion.

- A GPS has a screen, which is unquestionably a distraction from the road ahead (and despite it providing audio instructions, we are compelled, like moths to a flame, to look at it).
- A GPS is not infallible, of course, and perhaps the only thing more dangerous than a distracted teen driver is a confused or lost teen driver.
- GPS voice commands direct us where and when to turn but may give the misleading impression that it is *safe* to turn, which may not be the case. In other words, we worry that for a teen driver, a voice command from a GPS may be taken (as illogical as it may sound) as the GPS's evaluation that the turn can be made safely, as if the GPS has also evaluated traffic surrounding the vehicle.
- The simple fact is that teen drivers are still learning to drive, and a GPS is one more thing to think about.

Taking all this into account, here are several recommendations for parents considering whether their teen driver should use a GPS:

- In general, for the reasons listed above, teen drivers should avoid using a GPS, if possible, even if it is technically legal.
- Don't let a GPS lull you or your teen into skipping one of the most important steps that should take place before a teen driver gets behind the wheel: planning the intended route. Put another way, do not under any circumstances think that using a GPS is a reason to allow your teen to jump into a car and drive to an unfamiliar place without planning because the GPS will show the way.

- If your teen intends to use a GPS, make its use a part of the teen's supervised training, so that he or she has experience with it when beginning to drive unsupervised.
- Emphasize to your teen that, if a GPS must be used, typing in the address must be done before the car is in motion; if the address needs to be revised, the teen should pull off the road into a safe place before doing so.

We should not even be debating whether teen drivers should use a GPS. It is surprising that teen driver laws don't ban GPS units as mobile electronic devices, and our antitexting laws (for everyone else) don't ban them, on the basis that they assist navigation. But just because a GPS is legal doesn't mean that it does not increase the already considerable dangers of teen driving.

Finally, we should not neglect auditory distraction as a form of distracted driving. As iPads, smartphones, and similar devices have proliferated, it is common to see drivers, especially younger ones, wearing earbuds or even full-size headphones (the latter not only provide sound but also are designed to block out most background noise) while driving. Tim once observed a young driver who was oblivious to an ambulance behind her, siren blaring, because she was listening to her iPod with earphones. In 2012 two teen drivers died in two separate crashes when wearing headphones contributed to their not hearing an oncoming train at a rail crossing. The danger is real. Ears are essential safety equipment that should not be blocked.

According to AAA's *Digest of State Motor Vehicle Laws*, only a few states expressly regulate or prohibit the use of headphones while driving. In fact, many state distracted driving laws specifically exempt "audio." That means using an electronic device with earbuds or headphones to play music, receive language instruction, listen to an audiobook, and so forth is perfectly legal. People who are hard of hearing are not prohibited from obtaining a driver's license, and in fact there are special driver's ed programs as well as apps and other technology to help drivers who have biological hearing loss.

For parents of teen drivers, then, we offer this important caution: don't let your teen drivers wear earbuds or headphones while driving, or play their music so loudly (that includes on the car audio system) that they hear nothing else. Purposely blocking off hearing while driving is a bad idea. Reduction or loss of hearing is a form of distracted driving because it reduces reaction time to circumstances that can cause a crash. And note that, with regard to this form of distraction, parents may not have state laws to back them up; they are often on their own in imposing this limitation. Teen drivers should be all ears, and parents should make sure they are.

20

Alcohol- and Drug-Impaired Driving

Impaired driving is a physical or mental condition that continuously—for hours at a time—slows or otherwise interferes with mental and therefore physical responses to the driving situation. Thus, intoxication or being under the influence of drugs directly elevate the risks of driving because the substances interfere with a driver's ability to safely operate a vehicle. In teens the danger is compounded by a lack of driving experience and the teenage brain which, as we explained earlier, simply doesn't recognize and respond to risk the same way an adult brain does.

All states and the District of Columbia have twenty-one-year-old minimum drinking age laws, which are credited with saving more than thirty thousand lives (all ages) since 1975. In fact, the number of teen drivers involved in fatal crashes who were found to have alcohol in their systems (referred to as blood alcohol concentration, or BAC level) dropped by nearly half over the past decade. Zero tolerance laws, school- and community-based education programs such as DARE (Drug Abuse Resistance Education) and SADD (Students Against Destructive Decisions), the national designated driver movement, and on-demand ride-sharing programs are all contributing to the reduction. Indeed, research suggests that today's teen drivers are far more likely to refrain from getting behind the wheel after drinking than their parents were when they were teens.

Even so, as parents we must remain vigilant when it comes to alcohol and driving, because nearly a quarter of teen drivers involved in fatal crashes over the past decade had a 0.01 BAC or higher, a statistic that has remained constant. Parents also need to know that teen males are twice as likely as teen females to test positive for alcohol in fatal crashes. That rate is even higher when comparing older (eighteen- to twenty-year-old) male and female teen drivers.

When it comes to drugs, the topic is a bit more complicated. That's because millions of teens today take a wide variety of medications, and these legally prescribed drugs may have a helpful, neutral, or harmful impact on driving ability. A stimulant, arguably, could make a driver more alert, while a sedative might lower a driver's anxiety. For this reason, parents and supervising adults should carefully evaluate, with a doctor's help, the potential effects of prescription or over-the-counter medications on driving. In our opinion, however, zero tolerance is the only acceptable stance when it comes to illegal drug use. Marijuana is the illicit drug most likely to be used by US teens, with nearly half of twelfth graders reporting using it at least once in their lifetime and nearly a quarter indicating use in the past thirty days. In Washington State, where marijuana has been legalized for recreational use (currently it is legal in eight states and the District of Columbia), safety officials indicate that one in four high school seniors are using marijuana and think that, unlike alcohol, it doesn't impair their ability to drive.

Moreover, marijuana is often viewed as a "gateway" drug, a prelude to chronic substance abuse. Studies indicate that if a teen uses marijuana before the age of sixteen and for a prolonged period of time, a number of developmental and social problems can result. Regarding driving, marijuana impairs performance and more than doubles a driver's risk of being involved in a crash. During the past decade, fatal crashes involving marijuana use have tripled, with increases reported for all age groups and both sexes.

As parents, we must be good role models, which includes not only refraining from driving under the influence of alcohol or drugs but also not relying on our new teen drivers (whether a permit or restricted license holder) to be our chauffeur. Several national programs help parents talk to their teens about alcohol and drugs: Mothers Against Drunk Driving's (MADD) Power of Parents program, the Foundation for Advancing Alcohol Responsibility's (FAAR) "I Know Everything" program, and the Partnership for Drug-Free Kids Parent Toolkit provide research-based tools to help parents start a dialogue.

We also offer the following best practices:

- Make sure your teen knows that it is illegal for anyone under the age of twenty-one to drink, and it is illegal for teens to drink and drive.
- Understand that, just as with driving habits, in your alcohol and drug use you are modeling conduct for your teen.
- Be in close contact with other parents or adults who are supervising your teen or should be.

- When negotiating a parent-teen driving agreement, spend time on the zero tolerance paragraph about alcohol and drug use.
- Discuss with your teen the technique for getting out of a car being driven by an impaired driver, such as "Please pull over and let me out; I'm about to throw up."
- As stated in the model parent-teen driving agreement, note especially the paragraph saying, "At any time and for any reason, I may call for a safe ride to avoid a dangerous situation" and "My reasons for requesting the ride will not be a violation of this agreement."

The challenges presented by alcohol and drug use are inextricably woven into numerous aspects of parenting, but the stakes are higher when the conduct at issue is driving drunk, high, or both.

21

Drowsy Driving

Sleep is not overrated—particularly when it comes to driving. Lack of sleep slows our reaction time, impairs judgment and awareness of what is happening around us, and increases lapses in attention and risk taking. It also can result in "micro sleep," when we unwittingly doze off for a few seconds while driving.

A sleep-deprived driver will experience performance deficits similar to those of someone who has been drinking. For example, a driver who hasn't slept in eighteen hours will mimic a 0.05 BAC; twenty-one hours without sleep is equivalent to 0.08 BAC, the legal limit in all states. This has prompted federal safety officials to expand the definition of impaired driving to include not only drunk, drugged, and distracted but also drowsy.

No one is immune from drowsy driving, but teens and young adults are particularly vulnerable. It's estimated that drivers twenty-five years of age and younger are involved in more than half of drowsy driving crashes annually. Teens' lack of driving experience coupled with biological changes that impact their sleep-wake cycle explain the increased risk. Their bodies' delayed secretion of melatonin, which causes sleepiness, along with an altered sleep drive result in teens staying awake later at night. The problem is teens still need at least eight and a half to nine and a half hours of sleep per night, which most simply aren't getting.

Insufficient sleep is slightly more problematic for teenage girls than boys, but it worsens for both sexes if they leave the household around age eighteen and are no longer under parental supervision. A study of college freshmen found that they go to sleep approximately seventy-five minutes later than they did as high school seniors, and pull all-nighters at least once a week. This, noted the researchers, causes "students [to] experience a social jet lag—the difference between week and weekend sleep schedules—equivalent to flying from New York to Denver and back every weekend."

This lack of sleep not only contributes to injury risk for teen drivers but also results in them being more likely to drink and drive, text while driving, ride with a driver who has consumed alcohol, and not buckle up. There are no laws requiring teen drivers to get a specified amount of rest before driving, although nighttime driving restrictions try to achieve this indirectly. Therefore, *sufficient sleep is probably the single most important factor affecting teen drivers that parents and supervising adults must reevaluate every day—and perhaps even twice a day.* In this area parents will need to make judgment calls because they simply may not be able to determine how tired their teen is.

The most critical thing parents must do is help their teens get a good night's sleep. Experts suggest the following:

- Establish a regular lights-out time, which includes a limit on using computers and other devices. This will force your teen to focus on getting homework done rather than using social media. Setting a firm limit also gives your teen an out with friends: "My parents are making me get off the computer at ten, so I have to get my homework done."

- Monitor your teen's extracurricular activities to guard against overscheduling that will make it difficult to relax and unwind. An overloaded schedule will likely cause your teen to have trouble falling asleep.

- Remove any device with a screen from the bedroom, and get your teen off screens two hours before bedtime. This may sound impossible, particularly since many teens use their phone as an alarm clock, but taking a cell phone to bed can prompt a teen to keep checking for messages and engage in conversations that delay and impair sleep.

- Keep tabs on caffeine. While teens are consuming less soda than they once did, they are dinking more coffee, tea, and energy drinks, which stay in their system for up to eight hours.

- Wake teens by 9:00 or 9:30 AM on the weekend. Yes, they will grumble, but catching up on sleep can cause a teen's body clock to shift, making it harder to get out of bed on the next school day.

When it comes to drowsy driving, parents must set clear rules, including insisting that teens be well rested before handing over the keys (this should be addressed in the parent-teen driving agreement); warning them about "looking out for the other guy" who may be doing something unsafe (to react, your teen has to be awake and alert); and recognizing when they are simply too tired to drive. The warning signs of fatigue include:

- frequent yawning or being unable to keep your eyes open
- daydreaming or having wandering, disconnected thoughts
- having trouble keeping your head up
- not remembering driving the last few miles
- ending up too close to cars
- missing road signs or driving past an intended turn or exit
- driving into another lane of traffic or onto a rumble strip (raised or grooved patterns that alert a driver by producing noise and vibration)

Discuss these warning signs with your teen and advise him to pull over to a safe place and take a nap if he experiences any of them—the only proven remedy for drowsy driving. (Also, be sure to practice what you preach.) While your teen might think rolling down a window, turning up the radio, or stopping for a caffeinated drink will renew alertness (it takes thirty minutes for caffeine to kick in), that is simply not the case.

The most important advice we can convey is this: be prepared to say no to your drowsy teen.

What Schools Can Do

While many parents may assume that late-night and bad-weather driving are the most hazardous times for teen drivers, research shows that the hours directly after school lets out are the most dangerous. If we think about it, this makes sense. Teens leaving school parking lots are the ones most likely to have illegal and distracting passengers, to be in a big hurry, and to be headed to a destination (a friend's house, a fast-food restaurant, and so on) that disqualifies the trip as "purposeful" driving. Teens leaving school may also be fatigued, resulting in drowsy driving.

If this phenomenon is true, then the exits from high school parking lots can be regarded as ground zero for safe teen driving, a place where time and effort spent encouraging awareness and enforcing safe driving rules will pay dividends in safety. So what can schools do to use parking lot exits as a control point for teen drivers?

One technique is signage—not just the familiar BUCKLE UP notices but also signs that convey more pointed messages. The best we've heard about is a series of four signs, large enough so teen drivers can't miss them, that convey these messages in this order:

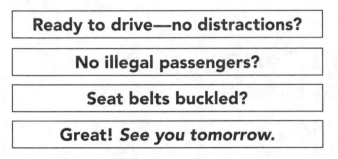

> ### Ready to drive—no distractions?
> ### No illegal passengers?
> ### Seat belts buckled?
> ### Great! *See you tomorrow.*

If your school's budget does not have funds for signs like these, encourage a PTA or even a shop class or service organization to step up.

Another technique is to spot-check cars leaving the parking lot. Police or a community relations officer could set up a formal roadblock, or a student group, PTA, or parent volunteers could conduct less formal checks. Violators could receive just a warning, especially with respect to passengers, but if the school is serious about compliance, the program can also involve reporting violators' license plates and additional stricter action—revoking a parking sticker or some in-school privilege for a period of time, for instance.

Surveillance cameras are another option. Many cities and towns, of course, are now installing such cameras at critical traffic locations to give drivers the message that violations will be recorded and prosecuted. Why not school parking lots? The danger is documented, so the cost should be justifiable.

Teen drivers leaving school parking lots are most likely to have illegal passengers on unexpected early dismissal days, such as when a snowstorm is approaching. On these days, parents, guardians, and others who are responsible for transporting teens home may not be able to do so, so teens grab a ride, whether legal and safe or not, with whoever can get them home quickest. Announcements (in school or online) about early dismissal should be accompanied by a reminder that rushing home to beat a storm is not a reason to violate safe teen driving passenger laws.

Schools and parent organizations can also help by encouraging and facilitating carpools with parent drivers, specifically as a way to prevent risky teen driving with passengers. After transporting kids to school, often in carpools, or putting them on a bus from kindergarten on, parents almost subconsciously yield to allowing peers to take over. Undoubtedly, convenience (and perhaps more sleep) for parents spurs this along. But parents should realize that they are not required to give up this role, and they can take it back immediately to avoid higher-risk situations such as bad weather or night transportation. The convenience of having teens drive should not take the place of parent-initiated carpools if that is the safer option.

What else can schools do to promote safer teen driving? Consider the following:

- Form a student-parent-faculty teen safe driving awareness group.
- Broadcast teen safe driving public service announcements over the PA system during school hours and at sporting events.
- Place teen safe driving reminder advertisements in programs handed out at high school sporting and other events.
- Sponsor a school-wide video or poster safe driving contest.

- Hang a teen safe driving banner in a strategic location on campus.
- Host a Teen Safe Driving Night with representatives from emergency medical services, law enforcement, driver training, and insurance. (Some schools require students to attend a teen driving night with a parent or guardian as a prerequisite for obtaining on-campus parking privileges following licensure.)
- Conduct an annual Teen Driving Awareness Day or Week.
- Incorporate teen safe driving into the school's health and wellness curriculum, and explore interdisciplinary opportunities (e.g., the physics of a car crash and what happens when you don't buckle up, the psychology of why we engage in unsafe behaviors, and the societal impacts of safe and unsafe driving).
- Invite guest speakers who can tell riveting personal stories (see chapter 12).
- Conduct an essay contest in a school publication.

Changing school start times is a proven way to allow teens to get more sleep, which reduces teen crashes (and has other beneficial educational effects). According to the American Academy of Pediatrics, which in 2014 called on schools to shift to an 8:30 AM or later start time for middle and high school students, "The research is clear that adolescents who get enough sleep have a reduced risk of being overweight or suffering depression, are less likely to be involved in automobile [crashes], and have better grades, higher standardized test scores and an overall better quality of life."

If your teen's school hasn't adopted a later start time, another long-standing practice should and can easily be changed. Every summer, most high schools send forms to parents and guardians that ask for permission with respect to transporting students to and from school activities. The forms usually look something like this:

☐ Yes ☐ No I give permission for my student to drive to and from school.

☐ Yes ☐ No I give permission for my student to ride to off-campus events/activities with other students as drivers.

☐ Yes ☐ No I give permission for my student to drive other students to off-campus events/activities.

This is usually the extent of the form, though sometimes it also asks if the student is authorized to drive a sibling to school, and sometimes whether the car the student will drive is insured.

The driving permission part of these forms, however, is a multipart invitation to trouble, because:

- the most dangerous hours for teen drivers are the hours directly after school lets out
- these "Yes/No" forms, if checked yes, allow your teen driver, with the school's blessing, to ride as a passenger with a driver unknown to you, and perhaps with other students in the car
- the forms rarely make any reference to the state's teen driving law and passenger restrictions; they can give the impression that off-campus events/activities are an exception to teen driver laws and passenger restrictions; and they not only encourage but also authorize a practice that we know is dangerous—teens driving with passengers

Why do schools use these forms? When teens drive, the school saves money on transportation and gas, no doubt. Another reason might be because the same form has been used for decades. Why do parents check yes? Well, the forms come from the school, so someone must have decided that students driving other students is safe, right?

In fairness, there is one aspect of the driving authorized by these forms that actually carries a lower risk. Most likely, one student transporting others to or from a school event would be "purposeful" driving. But this is the only counterweight to an otherwise dangerous practice.

What should schools and parents do? The safest option would be to not allow high school students to drive other students to school events, period. If transportation is needed, buses should be used or parents should be the drivers. Barring this complete prohibition, schools can:

- remind parents on the forms themselves what the state's passenger rules are (for example, "Our state prohibits teen drivers from carrying non–family members as passengers for one year after licensing")
- remind students and parents on a case-by-case basis when their transportation to and from a school event will involve a teen driver
- ask coaches and other supervisors of activities that occur outside of regular school hours to make sure they hand off their students to a safe ride home
- bar any teen who has received a ticket, citation, or license suspension from driving other students (which, of course, requires the teen or parents to notify the school)

- have each teen driver sign a school version of a parent-teen driver agreement
- include in back-to-school packets information about adherence to your state's GDL provisions and motor vehicle laws, and consequences for noncompliance
- remind every student who will be a passenger of a teen driver of the importance of a distraction-free car, the use of safety belts, and getting out of the car if the driver engages in unsafe driving

23

Blind Zones

A teen, at home, suddenly realizes that she is late—for school, sports, an activity, a community event, a family gathering, a date. She races into the kitchen, grabs the car keys from the basket, jumps into the car, starts the engine, and starts backing down the driveway.

And she doesn't look to see if anything or anyone is behind the vehicle, and so doesn't see the toddler playing in the driveway.

This stomach-turning scenario is not too difficult to envision, is it?

Every week in the United States, approximately fifty children are backed over by vehicles because they could not be seen by the driver. In some cases, the driver carefully checked the blind zones before getting into the vehicle, but then a toddler wandered into the zone just as the car started rolling. In other words, not every back-over is the result of carelessness, but all are a result of the fact that there are places that drivers cannot see.

Educating the public about blind zones is part of the mission of KidsAndCars.org. Teens, and of course the rest of us, need to be reminded about blind zones, which are one of those safety risks that lie just below the surface of our consciousness.

KidsAndCars.org features photos and illustrations of the danger. Every vehicle has blind zones in front and behind, with a bigger blind zone behind. The exact length, width, and height of the zone varies with the height of the driver, the elevation of the driver's seat, and the design of the vehicle, but the area can be anywhere from twenty to sixty feet long. Obviously, SUVs, light trucks, and cars with low suspensions have the biggest potential blind zones. In recent years, the number of blind zone incidents has increased dramatically, which is likely the result of more SUVs and light trucks being driven by the American public.

Technology is becoming part of the answer here. Some new cars have a backup camera, and this feature is expected to become standard on most cars in the next few years. Older vehicles can be retrofitted with backup cameras. However, these devices don't see everything and can distract the driver from checking the sides of the vehicle.

There is no magic solution. Explain to your teen what a blind zone is and point out approximately how large it is in the front and rear of each car your teen may drive. Then direct your teen to KidsAndCars.org to view the illustrations and read some of the harrowing stories of drivers who started their vehicles rolling.

Teens also need to understand the blind zones of big trucks. They're referred to as "no-zones"—places where a truck driver simply can't see other vehicles. The Commercial Vehicle Safety Alliance's Teens and Trucks program (see Teen Driving Resources, page 140) is designed to help teens safely share the road with big rigs and buses. The program addresses the rule of thumb for staying out of the no-zones: if you can't see the driver's mirrors, the driver can't see you. Moreover, large trucks make wider turns and take longer to stop.

Nearly 70 percent of crashes involving large trucks and cars are the fault of the car drivers. Teens and young adults are particularly susceptible; they fail to recognize that trucks and cars have different handling characteristics. Make time during your teen's supervised practice to have them drive on roadways with big trucks.

Vehicle Identification Stickers

A hotly debated topic in teen driver safety is a system by which law enforcement and other drivers may identify a vehicle being driven by a teen. The system already exists in the sense that driver's ed cars usually carry a STUDENT DRIVER sign. The currently debated idea is to have teens display a sticker or decal somewhere on or within the vehicle when they are driving unsupervised by an instructor. The United Kingdom has done this for years, requiring new drivers to display an "L" (for Learner) in the rear window. An identifier is also used in several other countries, including Australia, Canada, Germany, Japan, and New Zealand.

Currently, New Jersey is the only state that has adopted this system, and there it occurred only after overcoming substantial opposition from elected officials and parents. The most common objections were that displaying a sticker might lead sexual predators to target solo teen drivers, especially girls, or might induce law enforcement to profile younger drivers. The principal argument in support of the decals is that police should be not only allowed but also encouraged to spotlight teen drivers because of their high crash rates, and that teen drivers will drive more responsibly if they know that law enforcement officials are capable of identifying their vehicles. (One way to identify cars driven by teens is to embed a sensor in the license plate or rear window that can be detected only by law enforcement—a technology that is feasible but not yet used in any state.)

New Jersey's decal requirement (implemented in 2010) has proven successful: crash rates have declined, law enforcement officers have embraced the tool, no teen driver has been accosted by a sexual predator, and the provision has not otherwise jeopardized the safety of teen drivers. (The decals are 1.5 inches by 1 inch, red, reflectorized, and removable with a Velcro-like sticker; they attach to the front and rear license plates.) While there was at first opposition among parents and teens after adoption, it has declined considerably, with more than 65 percent of parents (surveyed in 2017) of sixteen- to twenty-year-olds saying they "will, do or did require their teen driver to display the decal while holding their permit and probationary license."

Identifying decals fit logically into GDL enforcement. As discussed in chapter 7, graduated driver licensing is first and foremost a parent program, but once teens pull out of the driveway on their own, parents aren't there to remind them to watch their speed, buckle up, or do the many other things that will keep them safe. Police officers are the next line of defense. They are tasked with making the stop if a teen violates a GDL restriction or other motor vehicle law that puts at risk not only that teen and his or her passengers but also anyone else on the road.

But teen driver laws are difficult for police to enforce if they can't identify vehicles driven by teens who hold a graduated driver license. Indeed, it is an anomaly that GDL laws are passed to impose special rules based on the age of the driver, but law enforcement officials have no way to detect which vehicles are subject to these rules. It makes little sense that we identify student drivers when they are in the car with an instructor but not when they drive without a supervising adult. With the results from New Jersey now part of the mix, we encourage other states to add a decal or identifier provision to their GDL law and parents to embrace this proven tool.

25

Defensive Driver Education as a Supplement

Most insurance companies provide a discount to teen drivers under twenty-one years of age who complete an approved driver education and training program. Some carriers also offer an insurance premium discount for completion of a defensive driving course. These courses may take the form of classroom or behind-the-wheel training, and include the use of computer-based simulators. In states where teen drivers are not required to complete driver education or training as a prerequisite for licensure (currently, less than half of states require this), classroom and defensive driving programs can help fill that void, but we caution parents against relying on these programs to replace formal education and training or supervised on-the-road practice. Instead, they should complement that training.

What should you look for in a defensive driving program? If you and your teen opt for a program delivered in a classroom setting, seek out training that is interactive, specifically designed for teen drivers, and facilitated by certified instructors. The training should not only help teens recognize the consequences for their driving actions but also provide tools to encourage them to make positive choices.

For behind-the-wheel training, look for programs that focus on helping teens build critical driving kills—hazard recognition, vehicle handling, and speed and space management, which are critical factors in more than 60 percent of teen driver crashes. Be sure to ask about the instructors' experience: Are they professionals who are experienced in working with teens? Also consider programs that include a parent component that will help you build upon what your teen learns during the course.

Whether you and your teen opt for a classroom or behind-the-wheel program, choose one that is endorsed by a reputable national safety organization such as the National Safety Council, Governors Highway Safety Association, or Students Against Destructive Decisions.

In addition to defensive driving courses, consider trying computer-based software programs and simulators specifically designed to help novice drivers identify risks and take appropriate action. Research suggests that this training can be helpful in improving teen risk-assessment and basic understanding of the dangers of distracted driving and other unsafe behavior. But there is also general agreement that more study is needed to determine if what teens learn is lasting and translates into action on the road.

Most experts say that what a teen driver needs most are defensive driving skills and the confidence to look beyond the perimeter of his or her own vehicle to the traffic situation ahead. As parents, it is our job to help our teens recognize why they are participating in this training—to become better, safer drivers.

26

Non-English-Speaking and Single-Parent Households

The problem of conveying health and safety information to non-English-speaking households is an enormous one, and it reaches far beyond safe teen driving. We can only summarize the basic elements of the problem. To convey safety warnings effectively, messages must be delivered not only in the listener's language but also in the correct dialect and in a culturally relevant manner. For example, in some cultures a predominant belief is that an individual has little control over life's occurrences. Such an attitude could undermine a take-charge message to parents of new drivers.

Teen driving in non-English-speaking households has become an important issue as several states, including populous ones like California and Florida, have allowed undocumented residents to obtain driver's licenses and have tackled the enormous challenge of licensing, registration, and driver education. Many of those residents covered by these new laws are Spanish speakers, though programs in Chinese, Japanese, Korean, French, and other languages have also been introduced.

For parents of teens in Spanish-speaking households, the first edition of this book, under the title *No Tan Rápido*, was published in 2015 and is available through bookstores and online.

Single-parent households present another challenge, illustrated by the following scenario we have both encountered in our respective states: A mother, divorced for several years from the father of her newly licensed teenage daughter, asked what to do when her ex-husband bought their daughter a car. The parents live in the same region and are in regular communication, but the father did not ask for the mother's consent before buying the car.

We offered each mother two pieces of advice. The first was to bring to the ex-husband's attention research showing that teen drivers with their own cars have higher crash rates than those who depend on shared cars (see chapter 18). Second, we suggested that each mother draft a parent-teen driving agreement and sit down with their teen and ex-spouse to discuss it, agree on it, and sign it as soon as possible.

Though each teen's driving between the custodial and noncustodial parent's home might be considered purposeful, the car purchase likely made it possible for the teens to drive more than they were ready to handle. Also, the noncustodial parent surprising the other parent by buying a car for their new teen driver raises a question about which parent is overseeing driving privileges and safety. Furthermore, it would seem that in this situation, the father could be characterized as putting convenience ahead of safety.

These circumstances—not uncommon, even in nondivorced families—call for even greater caution and conversation, with decisions about each teen's driving to be made day by day. A parent-teen driving agreement signed by each teen's parents would be a good start.

27

Supervising Other People's Teens

You observe a teen driver you know—from school, sports, a community activity, the neighborhood—speeding, texting, drag racing, carrying passengers you know are illegal, or driving after the state's curfew. Do you inform the teen driver's parent or guardian?

Your own teen reports seeing others at his school leaving the parking lot with friends whose presence violates the state's passenger restrictions. He also knows this group is going to be unruly and dangerous. Should he inform someone at school? Should you? When it comes to teen drivers, are parents the keepers of other people's kids?

The obstacles that a parent would face in alerting the parent of a teen who was observed driving illegally or dangerously are easy to catalog. To begin with, there is the possibility that the teen's parent does not understand the dangers of teen driving, and so may respond with indifference to your "I saw Billy texting while driving." The parent may reply with a stern warning to "mind your own business" or perhaps a snotty question about whether your own driving or your teen's is so perfect that you have now been appointed community watchdog. Maybe the parent will get defensive because the behavior you witnessed is something this parent does routinely, so your comment is a complaint about not only the teen's driving but also the parent's. And in these days of social media posts that can go viral in seconds, there's the fear that a complaint about another parent's teen driver will end up shared on Facebook or Twitter. What started out as a well-intentioned, one-to-one alert could suddenly have you vilified as a goody-two-shoes or a tattletale.

Yes, it is easy to list the reasons why you shouldn't even consider being an informant about another family's teen driver. Yet there are just as many reasons why you should.

Safe teen driving is everyone's concern, for the simple and well-documented reason that teen drivers crash three times more frequently than the safest age group of drivers, thirty-five- to forty-nine-year-olds; and when they do, they injure or kill many more people than only themselves. Every year in our country, three million teens get their licenses; they share the road with all of us. The safety of every driver and passenger is more in jeopardy with teen drivers than with any other age group. And this is before we factor in distraction, alcohol and drug use, speeding, drowsy driving, and other unsafe behaviors that compound that risk.

Next, please ask yourself: If your teen driver was doing something dangerous, would you want to be informed, regardless of the source? Hopefully your quick and unhesitating answer is yes.

Let's also remember that the police simply cannot be everywhere or even most places we need them, so supervision of teen drivers is primarily up to parents. (And as we pointed out in chapter 7, GDL, the most effective tool we have for helping teen drivers overcome risk, is first and foremost a parent program.) To say that this responsibility is limited to watching over your own teen driver is to draw an unnecessary line and to open up a gap in the supervision that is essential for safe teen driving.

Finally, please note that with teen drivers, time is the enemy. If teen drivers misbehave and get away with it, they are empowered to act the same way again or even to push the envelope further. It is well documented that teen driver attitudes deteriorate in the first six months after they obtain their licenses, when the lessons and cautions of driver's ed and the learner's permit stage are easily forgotten and the inherent teen attraction to risk-taking kicks in. Bad or illegal driving observed but unreported is not just an omission but also a refusal to act on behalf of public safety.

Everything considered, we owe it to our families, our communities, and ourselves to promptly report information about teen driver misconduct to a parent, guardian, school official, or whoever is most appropriate to act.

This leaves us with two issues: how best to communicate, and what to say? As to how to do it, the options are face-to-face conversation, a phone call, an e-mail, or a text message. This is a judgment call. The problem with an e-mail or a text, of course, is that it may get forwarded somewhere that you can't control and don't want it to be, and this may be a deterrent ("Look at what this guy said about my son!"). A face-to-face visit may compress the fears listed above. A phone call may be the safest way.

We offer the following script for calling another parent to report their teen driver's illegal or dangerous behavior:

This is Jane from Jones Road. I want to apologize in advance for this call and hope you will understand why I am calling. I saw your son texting while driving on Hope Street. It made me very concerned for his safety and those driving nearby. [Here, you can insert a compliment about the teen: "He is such a great young man."] Again, I hope you're not offended by my bringing this up. I'm doing this out of concern for safety. I appreciate you taking my call.

At the risk of using a cliché, when it comes to safe teen driving, it definitely takes a village. So please don't be afraid to call, and don't delay.

28

In Summary:
Tips from Tim and Pam

1. Keep in mind that there is no such thing as a safe teen driver, primarily because the part of the human brain that provides judgment and restraint does not fully develop until the early to midtwenties, and no amount of training can overcome this limitation.

2. Remember that a graduate of driver's ed is a beginner, not a safe or experienced driver.

3. Recognize that enforcement of teen driving laws is primarily up to parents and guardians; police and schools can only help.

4. Make handing over the car keys a big deal every time by asking important questions (where, who, when) and reinforcing the rules.

5. Don't push a teen who, for whatever reason, is not ready to drive or capable of doing so safely; remember that a state's licensing age is not based on evidence that driving at age fourteen, fifteen, or sixteen is safe.

6. Prepare, sign, and enforce a parent-teen driving agreement.

7. Recognize the factors that substantially increase the already-high risk of a teen driver getting in a crash: speeding, drugs and alcohol, fatigue, bad weather, or an unsafe vehicle.

8. Recognize the difference between purposeful and recreational driving.

9. Understand that each passenger in a teen's car increases the likelihood of a crash, including siblings.

10. Demand full seat belt compliance by every teen driver and every passenger.

11. Recognize the first six months of solo driving as the most dangerous, and look for opportunities to continue to drive with your teen.

12. Don't let a teen be the primary or only driver of a car, and in any event, choose a car with the most safety features.

13. Be aware of the most dangerous times for teen drivers: after school lets out, 9:00 PM to midnight, and summer.

14. If a teen receives a ticket or citation, make her take her medicine without argument or delay.

15. Have zero tolerance for a teen driver using an electronic device, including a GPS, to text, type, read, watch video, or make a phone call, and refrain from calling or texting a teen who you know is driving.

16. Don't allow your teen to wear earbuds or headphones while driving.

17. Beware of school transportation forms that allow teens to carry passengers.

18. If you can afford one of the technologies that track your teen's driving, buy and install it, but do so with your teen's knowledge, if not acceptance.

19. Be responsible for all teen drivers you come in contact with, not just yours.
20. Don't put your convenience ahead of safety.
21. Be a good role model: avoid distractions, buckle up, obey speed limits, get plenty of sleep, never drive after drinking or using drugs, and be a defensive driver.
22. Don't be afraid to say no.

AFTERWORD

A Plea to Parents

FROM TIM

In the weeks and months after my son Reid's crash, I was less haunted by the feeling that I had made a terrible mistake in supervising my son's driving and more confused by the sense that I had done what parents are supposed to do—and he still died. I thought I was a reasonably well-informed, hands-on, mainstream parent.

I wasn't. Not even close. As my story in chapter 1 reveals, I made plenty of mistakes, because—like too many parents—I did not understand the dangers or the steps I could take to counteract them. I thought driver's ed had made Reid a relatively safe driver and that getting his license from our DMV was further confirmation. I didn't act like an air traffic controller. We didn't sign a parent-teen driving agreement. I allowed him to buy his own car and then to take it to hang out with his friends.

I signed a form allowing him to drive others to and from school activities. I didn't understand the dangers of cell phones or texting. In my defense, he drove a relatively safe car crash-free for eleven months, and on the night he died, he took the car on an unauthorized joyride with passengers. Alcohol, drugs, fatigue, his cell phone, and his passengers played no role in his crash, and it's a fact that an eighteen-inch change in where his car hit the guardrail would have spared his life when speed and inexperience caused him to lose control.

I don't beat myself up anymore about what happened. I didn't give him the keys on the night of December 1, 2006. I didn't OK his route or passengers, and no parent can supervise a teen driver 24/7. Occasionally I count my blessings: Reid's crash didn't kill anyone else.

I am left to convey this message to parents: Be better than I was. Learn from my experience and homework, and resolve to avoid my mistakes.

From Pam

With Zach, despite all I knew about safe teen driving and the steps I took to be an authoritative, safety-conscious parent, I couldn't overcome the two things that impact every teen driver's safety: inexperience and an immature brain. Not even being the Safety Mom could guarantee that Zach would drive crash-free. He survived both crashes, and today he continues to gain experience and skill every time he drives. But at age twenty-two, Zach isn't over the safety hurdle yet, and I continue to exercise my parental right to drive with him every chance I get and to make his safety my highest priority.

From Both of Us

We recognize that following the advice in this book is not a guarantee of safety, and we understand that parenting teens is a balancing act of teaching them about danger by exposing them to it and pulling them back or saying no when the situation becomes too risky. So we urge you:

- use utmost caution
- understand how unalterably dangerous teen driving is
- don't put convenience ahead of safety
- be proactive each and every day
- preempt the riskiest situations
- let the tether out in very small increments
- if your gut says that a particular drive is a bad idea, go with your instinct, not peer pressure
- don't befriend your teen with car keys

The consequences of a teen driver fatality or serious injury are beyond the scope of this book, and we aim to offer only best practices, not promises. But the steps we advocate here are proven ways for you and your family to better manage the risks of teen driving and to avoid the unthinkable.

Thanks for listening.

Teen Driving Resources

AAA Foundation for Traffic Safety, which includes in-depth research on teen driving and instruction: www.aaafoundation.org

Allstate Foundation, which promotes the use of parent-teen driver agreements: www.allstatefoundation.org/teen_safe_driving.html

Centers for Disease Control and Prevention's Safe Teen Driving: www.cdc.gov/Features/TeenDrivers

Commercial Vehicle Safety Alliance's Teens and Trucks, whose program is designed to help teens safely share the road with trucks and buses: http://cvsa.org/program/programs/operation-safe-driver/teens-and-trucks

Ford's Driving Skills for Life program, which offers ride and drive defensive driver training to teens and parents: www.drivingskillsforlife.com

Governors Highway Safety Association, which details the GDL requirements by state and features reports addressing teen safe driving topics and drowsy driving (authored by Pam): www.ghsa.org

Impact Teen Drivers, a Sacramento, California–based coalition
of parents, law enforcement, and first responders
that provides innovative training programs: www
.impactteendrivers.org

Insurance Institute for Highway Safety, a national leader in
researching all aspects of traffic safety, including best cars
for teens: www.iihs.org

Kia's *B.R.A.K.E.S* (Be Responsible and Keep Everyone Safe):
https://putonthebrakes.org

Liberty Mutual Insurance, offering parent and teen tips and
tools: www.libertymutual.com/auto/car-insurance-for
-teens

Lifesavers National Conference on Highway Safety Priorities;
the annual conference offers a slate of teen driving
workshops: http://lifesaversconference.org

MADD's underage drinking prevention program, which
includes a specific section on teen driving: www.madd.org
/the-solution/power-of-parents

Mourning Parents Act, Inc., a Connecticut-based organization
of parents who have lost children in automobile crashes
(Tim is a participant); the group brings a message, in
person, to high school students about the consequences
for families of unsafe driving: www.mourningparentsact
.org

MyCarDoesWhat.org, developed by the National Safety
Council, helps drivers understand the safety technology in
their vehicles: https://mycardoeswhat.org

National Highway Traffic Safety Administration (NHTSA),
the US government's comprehensive list of vehicle safety
ratings: www.safercar.gov

National Organizations for Youth Safety (NOYS), a national
coalition of groups whose mission involves all aspects of
youth safety and safe teen driving in particular. NOYS is
active in combating texting and distracted driving among
teen drivers. "Under Your Influence" is the organization's
safe teen driving monthly e-newsletter: https://noys.org;
www.underyourinfluence.org

National Safety Council, which provides teen safe driving
information, resources, and coaching tips for parents via
the website: www.driveithome.org

National Safety Council's Alive at 25, one of the most widely
delivered classroom teen defensive driving programs: www
.nsc.org/learn/Safety-Training/Pages/teen-young-adult
-defensive-driving-courses.aspx

Parents Central, the NHTSA's website for parents: www
.safercar.gov/parents/index.htm

State Farm Teen Driver Safety: http://teendriving.statefarm.com

Street Safe, based out of North Carolina: http://streetsafeus.com

Students Against Destructive Decisions (SADD), which
includes educational and prevention materials for students
to use in their schools and communities, as well as
information for parents, teachers, and other adults: www
.sadd.org

Teen Driver Source, from the Children's Hospital of Philadelphia,
a national leader in teen safe driving research; it features a
section expressly for parents: www.teendriversource.org

TeenDrive365, Toyota's teen driver program: www.toyota.com
/teendrive365

Teen Safe Driving Coalition partners with parents, teens, law
enforcement officials, driver education professionals, traffic
safety advocates, government agencies, and community
members to promote the proven principles of GDL: www
.teensafedriving.org

US Department of Transportation website that summarizes
current research about distracted driving: www.distraction
.gov

MODEL PARENT-TEEN DRIVING AGREEMENT

Driving is the leading cause of death and injury for those under age 24. Parent-teen driving agreements are a proven way to reduce crash risk. Complete and sign this Agreement when the teen obtains a learner's permit, and review and re-sign when the teen obtains a license.

Cautions for Parents and Supervising Adults

- State laws allow teens to obtain a learner's permit, but parents and guardians may prohibit those under 18 from starting to drive. *Review the safety risks stated below and use your judgment.*
- You are a *role model for your teen driver* and need to teach safe driving habits by being a responsible, defensive driver at all times.

Safety Risks of Teen Driving

- Driving is especially dangerous for teens because *the human brain does not fully develop* its ability to assess risk and danger *until we reach age 22 to 25; no amount of driver training can overcome this risk.*
- A teen driver violating state laws can cause *injury or death to people and damage to property, which can result in criminal and civil penalties and financial liability for parents or guardians.*

- Driver education is essential, but passing a course and obtaining a license only means that a teen is a beginner at a dangerous task; *it does not mean that the teen is a safe driver.*
- Speeding, reckless driving, alcohol or drug use, not using seat belts, distracting electronic devices, teen passengers, and fatigue *risk the life of the driver, passengers, other drivers, passengers in other vehicles, and pedestrians.*

TEEN DRIVER AGREEMENTS

1. Time Period: This Agreement will remain in effect until (*recommended: one year from initial license, or 18th birthday, whichever is later*) _____.

2. Parents/Supervising Adults: My driving will be supervised by a parent or supervising adult who will decide, day-by-day, whether it is safe for me to drive.

3. Driving Plan: I will get permission from one of my supervising adults every time I drive, and we will agree on my destination, route, time of departure and return, and passengers. Joyriding (driving with no destination or purpose) is not allowed.

4. Seat Belts: I will wear my seat belt, and I will make sure that every passenger in my car, of any age, wears one.

5. Speeding and Rules of the Road: I will obey speed limits, stop signs, traffic signals, and the rules of the road. I will drive at a reasonable speed and will reduce my speed when road conditions require (e.g., weather, darkness, sharp turns, hills, visibility, congestion, unfamiliar roads).

6. Cell Phones and Electronic Devices: Unless my vehicle is in park, I will not use any electronic device, whether in hand-held, hands-free, or voice-activated mode, for any purpose not related to the safe operation of the vehicle. Specifically, I will not use an electronic device to send or read a text message; send or view a photo or video; or make a phone call or communicate with a person outside the vehicle.

7. Curfews: I will not drive between the hours of (*fill in state curfew or stricter hours*) _____, except for (*fill in state law exceptions—school, job, medical, religious*) _____ _____. If I need to rely on an exception, I will get written permission and carry it in my vehicle.

8. Passengers (*must be consistent with state law; may be stricter; recommend three stages*): For my first ____ months with a license, I will carry only an adult who is supervising my driving. When I have had my license for _____ months, I will carry only a supervising driver and immediate family. I will not transport anyone else until I have had my license for _____.

9. Alcohol or Drug Use, Fatigue: I will never drive under the influence of alcohol or illegal or impairing drugs, or when, due to insufficient rest, I may not be able to maintain the focus needed to drive safely.

10. Violation Reporting; Suspension of Driving Privileges: Violations of this Agreement or state laws may be reported to one of my supervising adults by law enforcement, neighbors, school personnel, or friends. *IF I VIOLATE ANY OF THESE OBLIGATIONS, MY DRIVING PRIVILEGES WILL BE SUSPENDED FOR _____ DAYS.* This suspension will be in addition to any fine, penalty, or suspension under state law. If I drive while my privileges are suspended, they will be suspended indefinitely.

11. Call for a Safe Ride: At any time and for any reason, I may call for a safe ride to avoid a dangerous situation. My reason for requesting the ride will not be a violation of this Agreement.

12. Costs of Driving: During this Agreement, my parents/ supervising adults and I will divide costs of insurance, gas, and maintenance as follows: _____.

13. Monitoring Technology: (*Specify any device that will be installed in the vehicle or used to track information about the teen's operation of the vehicle.*) _____.

14. Mediator (*optional*): We appoint _____ to serve as mediator. If a dispute arises about this Agreement, we will ask our mediator for advice. (Contact number: _____ _____).

15. Other Agreements: _____
_____
_____

BY SIGNING BELOW, WE COMMIT OURSELVES TO SAFETY.

_____   _____

Teen Driver   Date

_____   _____

Parent/Supervising Adult   Date

_____   _____

Parent/Supervising Adult   Date

Keep one copy in a visible place at home and one copy in the vehicle glove box.

ACKNOWLEDGMENTS

FROM TIM

In 2006, I would have given everything I have to save my son and avoid the pain that followed his passing. But counting my blessings, I gratefully acknowledge the people without whom this book would not have been written.

First and foremost, thanks to my daughter Martha for being my partner in honoring Reid's memory.

Thank you to Christina Steinhauser for her loving support as well as an insightful edit of this second edition that made it more user friendly to parents.

This book was originally the suggestion of my college classmate and publishing industry veteran Kathy Mintz. She saw before I did that my blog had accumulated enough content and national interest to warrant a handbook. Matt Richtel of the *New York Times* provided specific inspiration, and the belief that I could make a difference, through his 2009–10 Pulitzer Prize–winning series on distracted driving.

My gratitude to Sandy Spavone, today the executive director of Family, Career and Community Leaders of America, and Nicole Graziosi. In early 2011, on the staff of the National Organization for Youth Safety, Sandy and Nicole embraced this project and energetically supported it.

Curt Clarisey of Simsbury, Connecticut, designed my blog and has faithfully maintained and improved it. He educated me about successful blogging. Curt, thank you for your tireless efforts.

Joy Tutela has been so much more than my agent: friend, confidante, adviser, and rock. Her unwavering belief in Reid's story as a way to help parents has kept me going.

It has been a joy to work with the folks at Chicago Review Press and Independent Publishers Group, especially editors Lisa Reardon and Ellen Hornor and marketing manager Mary Kravenas.

My assistant of twenty-three years, Erin Fitzgerald, has typed and formatted countless revisions of this manuscript and has done so always with her ever-present cheerfulness.

Thanks to attorney Robert Labate for his help with legal matters. Cathy Gillen of the Gillen Group graciously allowed me to benefit from her incomparable knowledge and contacts in the traffic safety and transportation communities.

Thank you to those in the national and New England automotive and traffic safety communities who edited or commented on the manuscript: Kevin Borrup and Garry Lapidus of Connecticut Children's Medical Center, Dr. Kelly Browning of California's Impact Teen Drivers, Sharon Silke Carty of the *Huffington Post*, Sherry Chapman of !MPACT, Cathy Gillen of the Road Safety Foundation, Bruce Hamilton of the Roadway Safety Foundation, Dean Johnson of the Sandy Wood Johnson Foundation, the late Dave Preusser of Preusser Research Group, and Piña Violano of Yale New Haven Hospital.

Thank you to the marketing department staff at Shipman & Goodwin LLP—Jill Mastrianni, Jen Stokes, and Maria

Ramsay—for their belief in my mission and expert support for my safe teen driving presentations. Thanks also to Shipman & Goodwin colleagues, Scott Murphy, Barry Hawkins, and Alan Lieberman, especially, for giving me encouragement and time to work on safe teen driving, and to support staff Jeanne Swayner, Carolyn Lawrence, Deanna Edwards, and Jessie Rodriguez for their tireless evening and weekend help.

In April 2013, a focus group drawn from attendees of the Lifesavers Conference on Highway Safety Priorities, ably led by Dr. Kelly Browning, provided invaluable feedback on the final draft of the first edition of this book. Thank you to Mi Ae Lipe, Rosalie Ashcraft, Ted Beckman, Kathy Bernstein, Lee Boan, Sgt. Matt Cabot, Leeana Clegg, Amanda Foster, Howard Hedegard, Herbert Homan, Lisa Kutis, Lorrie Lynn, Pam Morrison, Susanne Ogaitis-Jones, Brian Pearse, Gordy Pehrson, Karen Pennington, David Resnick, Jackie Stackhouse Leach, Richard Sullivan, Margaret Skrzypkowski, Donna Tate, Dana Teramoto, and Stacey Tisdale.

Thank you, finally, to my friends in the Connecticut and national traffic safety communities: Michelle Anderson, Ernie Bertothy, Dr. Brendan Campbell, Neal Chaudhary, Jenny Cheek, Hilda Crespo, Joe Cristalli, Mario Damiata, Diana Imondi Dias, Dr. Bella Dinh-Zarr, Brendan Dufor, Janette Fennell, Joel Feldman and Dianne Anderson, Ami Ghadia, Rep. Tony Guerrera, Richard Hastings, Jim Hedlund, Donna Jenner, Peter Kissinger, Gary Knepler, Jill Konopka, Jim MacPherson, Justin McNaull, Erin Meluso, Kelly Murphy, Janice Palmer, Starrla Pennick, Gordy Pehrson, Bill Seymour, Joe Toole, Col. Paul Vance, and Faith Voswinkel.

And, of course: thank you, Pam. Your incomparable knowledge of safe driving in general and teen driving in particular, as well as your passion, friendship, and energy, have convinced me to continue with my advocacy.

I am blessed many times over.

FROM PAM

I met Tim more than seven years ago while attending a driver education conference in Portland, Maine. I was invited to speak about teen driving with a particular focus on parent involvement. Following my presentation, many in attendance took the time to personally thank me for making the drive from New Jersey to share my expertise. Tim was one of those audience members, making it a point to introduce himself and share his story.

I'd met and worked with other parents who lost a teen in a car crash, but Tim was different. He wasn't just a grieving parent who wanted to tell his story but also a passionate, articulate, and motivated father who wanted to do something that truly got parents' attention. We kept in touch after that first meeting. Tim served on the expert panel for a report I researched and wrote on parental involvement for the Governors Highway Safety Association, and we made it a point to connect at regional and national safety conferences. When Tim decided to compile his driving blogs into a book, he asked me to read and critique what was the first draft of *Not So Fast*. He hoped it wasn't too much of an imposition; I was humbled by the request.

I read the manuscript, then read it again and realized that what Tim had to say needed to be heard by every parent—and well before their teens start to drive. I provided my comments and suggested edits and was honored to be quoted on the book's back cover. But what truly overwhelmed me was when Tim invited me to be the keynote speaker at the book launch at his family's church in Connecticut.

I became a cheerleader for *Not So Fast* and distributed hundreds of copies to parents and driver education professionals in New Jersey, where I live, and in other states. I've also used the bully pulpit provided to me through my writing and speaking to urge not only parents to read this book, but also anyone who interacts with teens. That's because despite having worked in traffic safety for three decades, I, like most other parents, still found myself shaking in my boots when my son began driving. What I loved about the first edition—and believe that we've stayed true to in the second—is that *Not So Fast* honestly and directly takes parents by the hand and lays out what they should be doing to help their teens survive their most dangerous years.

Thank you, Tim, for being a part of not only my teen driving and traffic safety professional life but also my personal life. We've both been through some significant life changes since we met, and I can't thank you enough for your friendship and support. I also want to thank you for allowing me to be a part of your more than decade-long journey to honor Reid's memory by sharing what we have learned about teen driving.

I owe a great deal of thanks to so many other people who have cheered me on as I endeavored to help teens be safe on the road and to educate parents about the critical role they play in that process. Thanks to my extended AAA family in New Jersey and across the nation—particularly Fred Gruel, Jennifer Schneider, Michele Mount, Judy Hartmann, Ed Baginski, Janet Ray, Garvin Kissinger, Bob Murry, Tom Crosby, Dan Beal, Ed Sharman (rest easy, dear friend), Mike Wright, Helen Schramek, Peter Kissinger—who were there when I started my traffic safety career and have taught me so much.

To former New Jersey governor Jon Corzine, Assemblyman John Wisniewski, the staff of the New Jersey Division of Highway Traffic Safety, the members of the New Jersey Teen Driver Study Commission, John Cichowiski (the Road Warrior), and an amazing community of traffic safety advocates, thank you for working collaboratively with me to strengthen the state's GDL law and keep teen driving front and center.

GHSA's Barbara Harsha and Jonathan Adkins, thank you for giving me the opportunity to write the first of what has become a series of teen driving reports when I was a fledgling consultant in need of work. I will always be grateful.

Thank you to the National Safety Council's teen driving team—especially Kathy Bernstein, Bridget Ballek, and Lorrie Lynn—for your help, guidance, and friendship. And to my fellow New Jersey Teen Safe Driving Coalition members, you inspire me each and every day to keep doing this important work. There are too many of you to list here, but I must call out Andy Anderson, Maureen Nussman, Wendy Berk, KJ Feury, Jackie Leach, Diana Starace, Susan Scarola, Roy Bavaro, Dan Gaskill, Chris Wagner, Jackie Malaska, and Donna Weeks.

Thank you to my high school English Enrichment teachers, Dr. Judith Ball Witmer and Nan Willis (rest in peace), and to Lebanon Valley College's Dr. Leon Markowitz (who is likely playing tennis in heaven when he's not reading Shakespeare) for teaching me to think critically and write clearly and succinctly.

To my parents—Polly and Dick Shadel—who taught me to never give less than 100 percent and to always be nice. I love you, Mom and Dad, and hope that I honor you through this work.

And lastly to Zach, thank you for being such a wonderful son. When you came into my life, I had no idea what it meant to love someone unconditionally. But through every one of your bumps, bruises, broken bones, and . . . car crashes, I came to realize that you are the love of my life, and I will do whatever it takes to keep you safe. Thanks for putting up with me—your safety mom. Growing up in the "safety spotlight" hasn't been easy, but you've handled it with grace, poise, and a smile on your face. I think you know how passionate I am about the work I do, but you are and will always be my most important work.

INDEX

ABOUT THE AUTHORS

Tim Hollister's seventeen-year-old son, Reid, died in a one-car crash on an interstate highway in central Connecticut in 2006. A year later, and after several other fatal crashes in the state, Connecticut's governor appointed Tim as a bereaved parent to a task force charged with reexamining the state's teen driver law. That task force led the state in 2008 to transform its law from one of the most lenient in the nation to one of the strictest. After serving on the task force, Tim began speaking and writing about topics largely unaddressed in the literature available to parents of teen drivers—what they can do before their teens get behind the wheel to preempt the most dangerous situations.

In 2009, Tim launched his national blog for parents of teen drivers, *From Reid's Dad* (www.fromreidsddad.org). The blog has been featured on *CBS Evening News with Scott Pelley* and has been covered by the *Huffington Post*, television and radio stations, newspapers, newsletters, websites, and other blogs and is now relied upon by parents, government agencies, driving schools, law enforcement, and traffic safety advocates across the country. In 2010 the National Highway Transportation Safety Administration honored Tim with its Public Service Award, the US Department of Transportation's highest civilian award for traffic safety. In 2014 and 2015 Tim received national public service awards from the Governor's Highway Safety Association and the National Safety Council. He is also the author of *His Father Still: A Parenting Memoir* (2015), which tells the story of Tim's parenting before and after Reid's fatal crash and examines how parents of teens must try to balance freedom with protection. In 2016 *His Father Still* was an Oprah's Book Club summer recommended reading selection.

Tim is a partner in a law firm in Connecticut, practicing land use and environmental law. For the past several years he has been listed among the *Best Lawyers in America*.

REID HOLLISTER
July 22, 1989–December 2, 2006

Pam Shadel Fischer is a transportation safety consultant with three decades of experience addressing behavioral safety issues at the local, state, and national level through advocacy, education, enforcement, policy, and planning. She cofounded the New Jersey Teen Safe Driving Coalition, a partnership with the National Safety Council that works to promote the proven principles of graduated driver licensing (GDL).

Pam has authored five national reports on teen driving for the Washington, DC–based Governors Highway Safety Association. She facilitated the nation's first Teen Driving Commission, composed entirely of teens, for the Georgia Highway Safety Office; developed Pennsylvania's first online teen safe driving resource guide; conducted a comprehensive review of Missouri's teen driving programs and policies; and serves as the legislative expert for an ongoing evaluation of New Jersey's GDL decal requirement known as Kyleigh's Law. Pam also regularly speaks about teen driving at state, regional, and national conferences and in the press.

Prior to forming her consulting firm, Pam served from 2007–2010 as Governor's Representative and Director of the New Jersey Division of Highway Traffic Safety. During that time, she chaired the New Jersey Teen Driver Study Commission, which prompted the passage of teen legislative initiatives that are credited with reducing crashes and fatalities involving teen drivers to historic lows. The commission's work was recognized with three national awards and held up as a model for other states.

Before leading the division, Pam was vice president of public affairs for the AAA New Jersey Automobile Club. She lobbied for proven traffic safety measures, including the state's GDL law, which took effect in 2001.

Her most important work, however, is partnering with her son, Zachary, to help him build skill and become a good driver for life.